Planetary
Influences
Sojourns &

Planetary Influences Sojourns

By Edgar Cayce

A.R.E. Press • Virginia Beach • Virginia

A.R.E. Press
215 67th Street
Virginia Beach, VA 23451-2061

ISBN 13: 978-0-87604-602-9 (trade pbk.)

Cover design by Richard Boyle

Contents

Introduction

E dgar Cayce (pronounced KAY-see) was born on a farm near
Hopkinsville, Kentucky, on March 18, 1877. As a child, he displayed
unusual powers of perception. At the age of six, he told his parents that
he could see and talk with "visions," sometimes of relatives who had
recently died, and even angels. He could also sleep with his head on his
schoolbooks and awake with a photographic recall of their contents,
even citing the page upon which the answer appeared. However, after
completing seventh grade, he left school, which was not unusual for
boys at that time.

When he was twenty-one, he developed a paralysis of the throat
muscles, which caused him to lose his voice. When doctors were unable
to find a physical cause for this condition, Edgar Cayce asked a friend to
help him re-enter the same kind of hypnotic sleep that had enabled
him to memorize his schoolbooks as a child. The friend gave him the
necessary suggestions, and, once he was in this trance state, Cayce spoke
clearly and directly without any difficulty. He instructed the "hypnotist"
to give him a suggestion to increase the blood flow to his throat; when
the suggestion was given, Cayce's throat turned blood red. Then, while
still under hypnosis, Cayce recommended some specific medication and

manipulative therapy that would aid in restoring his voice completely.

On subsequent occasions, Cayce would go into the hypnotic state to diagnose and prescribe healing for others, with much success. Doctors around Hopkinsville and Bowling Green, Kentucky, took advantage of Cayce's unique talent to diagnose their patients. They soon discovered that all Cayce needed were the name and address of a patient to "tune in" telepathically to that individual's mind and body. The patient didn't have to be near Cayce; he could tune in to the person wherever he or she was.

When one of the young MDs working with Cayce submitted a report on his strange abilities to a clinical research society in Boston, the reactions were amazing. On October 9, 1910, *The New York Times* carried two pages of headlines and pictures. From then on, people from all over the country sought "The Sleeping Prophet," as he was to be known.

The routine he used for conducting a trance diagnosis was to recline on a couch, hands folded across his solar-plexus, and breathe deeply. Eventually, his eyelids would begin fluttering, and his breathing would become deep and rhythmical. This was the signal to the conductor (usually his wife, Gertrude) to make verbal contact with Cayce's subconscious by giving a suggestion. Unless this procedure was timed to synchronize with his fluttering eyelids and the change in his breathing, Cayce would proceed beyond his trance state and simply fall fast asleep. However, once the suggestion was made, Cayce would proceed to describe the patient as though he or she were sitting right next to him, his mind functioning much as an x-ray scanner, seeing into every organ of the person's body. When he was finished, he would say, "Ready for questions." However, in many cases his mind would have already anticipated the patient's questions, answering them during the main session. Eventually, he would say, "We are through for the present," whereupon the conductor would give the suggestion to return to normal consciousness.

If this procedure were in any way violated, Cayce would be in serious personal danger. On one occasion, he remained in a trance state for three days and had actually been given up for dead by the attending doctors.

At each session, *or reading*, a stenographer (usually Gladys Davis

Turner, his personal secretary) would record everything Cayce said. Sometimes, during a trance session, Cayce would even correct the stenographer's spelling. It was as though his mind were in touch with everything around him and beyond.

Each client was identified with a number to keep his or her name private.

It was August 10, 1923, before anyone thought to ask the "sleeping" Cayce for insights beyond physical health – questions about life, death, and human destiny. In a small hotel room in Dayton, Ohio, Arthur Lammers asked the first set of philosophical questions that were to lead to an entirely new way of using Cayce's strange abilities. It was during this line of questioning that Cayce first began to talk about reincarnation as though it were as real and natural as the functionings of a physical body. This shocked and challenged Cayce and his family. They were deeply religious people, doing this work to help others because that's what their Christian faith taught. As a child, Cayce began to read the Bible from front to back and did so for every year of his life. Reincarnation was not part of the Cayce family's reality. Yet the healings and help continued to come. So the Cayce family continued with the physical material but cautiously reflected on the strange philosophical material. Ultimately, the Cayces began to accept the ideas, though not as *reincarnation*, per se. Edgar Cayce preferred to call it "the continuity of life." He felt that the Bible did contain much evidence that life, the true life in the Spirit, is continual.

Eventually, Edgar Cayce, following advice from his own readings, moved to Virginia Beach, Virginia, and set up a hospital where he continued to conduct his physical readings for the health of others. But he also continued this new line of readings called life readings. From 1925 through 1944, he conducted some 2,500 of these life readings, casually describing the past lives of individuals as though everyone believed reincarnation to be a reality. Such subjects as deep-seated fears, mental blocks, vocational talents, innate urges and abilities, marriage difficulties, child training, etc., were examined in the light of what the readings called the "karmic patterns" resulting from previous lives experienced by the individual's soul on the Earth plane.

When he died on January 3, 1945, in Virginia Beach, he left 14,256 documented stenographic records of the telepathic-clairvoyant readings he had given for more than 6,000 different people over a period of 43 years, consisting of 49,135 pages. The readings constitute one of the largest and most impressive records of psychic perception. Together with their relevant records, correspondence, and reports, they have been cross-indexed under thousands of subject headings and placed at the disposal of doctors, psychologists, students, writers, and investigators who still come to examine them. Of course, they are also available to the general public in books as well as on DVD ROM for Windows and Macintosh computers.

The Association for Research and Enlightenment (A.R.E.) was founded in 1931 to preserve these readings. As an open-membership research society, it continues to index and catalog the information, initiate investigation and experiments, and conduct conferences, seminars, and lectures. The A.R.E. also has the second largest and finest library of parapsychological and metaphysical books in the world, second only to the Vatican Library.

Language of the Edgar Cayce Discourses

Edgar Cayce dictated all of his discourses from a self-induced trance. A stenographer took his discourses down in shorthand and later typed them. Copies were sent to the person or persons who had requested the psychic reading, and one was put into the files of the A.R.E.

In his normal consciousness, Edgar Cayce spoke with a Southern accent but in the same manner as any other American. However, from the trance state, he spoke in the manner of the King James Bible, using "thees" and "thous." In trance, his syntax was also unusual. He put phrases, clauses, and sentences together in a manner that slows down any reader and requires careful attention in order to be sure of his meaning. This caused his stenographer to adopt some unusual punctuation in order to put into sentence form some of the long, complex thoughts conveyed by Cayce while in trance. Also, many of his discourses are so jam-packed with information and insights that it requires one to slow down and read more carefully in order to fully understand what he is intending.

From his trance state, Cayce explained that he got his information from two sources: 1) the inquiring individual's mind, mostly from his or her deeper, subconscious mind and 2) from the Universal Consciousness, the infinite mind within which the entire universe is conscious. He explained that every action and thought of every individual makes an impression upon the Universal Consciousness, an impression that can be psychically read. He correlated this with the Hindu concept of an Akashic Record, which is an ethereal, fourth-dimensional film upon which actions and thoughts are recorded and can be read at any time.

When giving one of his famous physical readings, Cayce acted as if he were actually scanning the entire body of the person, from the inside out. He explained that the subconscious mind of everyone contains all of the data on the condition of the physical body it inhabits, and Cayce simply connected with the patient's deeper mind. He could also give the cause of the condition, even if it was from early childhood or from many lifetimes ago in a previous incarnation of the soul. This was knowable because the soul remembers all of its experiences. He explained that deeper portions of the subconscious mind are the mind of the soul, and portions of the subconscious and the soul are in the body with the personality.

In life readings and topic readings, Cayce also connected with the subconscious minds of those inquiring, as well as with the Universal Consciousness.

Occasionally, Cayce would not have the material being requested, and he would say, "We do not have that here." This implied that Cayce's mind was more directed than one might think. He was not open to everything. From trance, he explained that the suggestion given at the beginning of one of his psychic readings so directed his deeper mind and focused it on the task or subject requested that he truly did not have other topics available. However, on a few occasions, he seemed able to shift topics in the middle of a reading.

The typed readings have a standard format. For privacy numbers were used in the place of the name of the person or persons receiving the reading, and a dash system kept track of how many readings the person had received. For example, reading 137-5 was the fifth reading for Mr. 137. Hypnotic material for Edgar Cayce is filed under the number 294. His first reading would be numbered 294-1, and each subsequent reading would increase the dash number (294-2, 294-3, and so on). Some numbers refer to groups of people, such as the Study Group, 262; and some numbers refer to specific research or guidance readings, such as the 254 series, containing the work readings dealing with the overall work of the organization that grew up around him, and the 364 and 996 series containing the readings on Atlantis. At the top of the reading are the reading number, the date and location, and the names or numbers of those in attendance. Occasionally, the stenographer would include a note about other conditions, such as the presence of a manuscript that the in-trance Cayce was supposed to view psychically and comment on. In most cases, I left in the entire format of a recorded reading, giving those present at the time, the location, date, and time of the reading, and any notes the stenographer may have made at the time. In some cases, only a paragraph or two were pertinent to our study, and in these cases, I give only the reading number.

As I explained, Cayce dictated all of these discourses while he was in trance. In most cases, he spoke in a monotone voice. However, he would often elevate his volume when saying a word or phrase. In these instances, his stenographer typed the words with all capital letters, to give the reader some sense of Cayce's increased volume. In many cases, these words appear to be rightly accentuated in Cayce's discourses. In other cases, it is unclear why particular words are capitalized.

Another style the stenographer adopted was to capitalize all of the letters in Cayce's many affirmations (positive-thought or prayer-like passages to be used by the recipient as a tool for focusing and raising consciousness). I changed these to upper- and lower-case letters, according to normal writing, and italicized them.

Whenever his stenographer was not sure that she had written down the correct word or might have missed or misunderstood a word, she inserted suggested words, comments, and explanations in brackets. If she knew of another reading that had similar material or that was being referred to during this reading, she would put the reading number in brackets. Within the text of a reading, all parentheses are asides made by Cayce himself while in trance not by his stenographer. She used brackets only within the text of a reading. In the preliminary material, she used parentheses in the normal manner. My comments are indicated by "Editor's Note."

A few common abbreviations used in these discourses were *GD* for

Gladys Davis, the stenographer; *GC* for Gertrude Cayce, Edgar's wife and the predominant conductor of the readings; *EC* for Edgar Cayce; and *Ass'n.* for the Association for Research and Enlightenment.

—John Van Auken, Editor

1

●

Eternally Celestial, Temporarily Terrestrial

Editor's Note: During his deep, meditative attunement to the Universal Consciousness, Edgar Cayce saw us as celestial beings, temporarily incarnating terrestrially. Here are some of his readings explaining this view.

Reading 136-83
. . . as [the entity] moves from sphere to sphere, seeks its way to the home, to the face of the Creator, the Father, the first cause . . .

Reading 5753-1
. . . [the goal is] that the created would be the companion for the Creator; that . . . [the entity seeks to] show itself to be not only worthy of, but companionable to, the Creator.

Reading 136-83
. . . self is lost in that of attaining for itself the nearer and nearer approach that buildeth in manifested form, whether in the Pleiades, Arcturus, Gemini, or in earth, in . . . Vulcan, or in Neptune . . . as light, a ray that does not end, lives on and on, until it becomes one in essence with the source of light.

Reading 311-2

As an entity passes on . . . from this present—or *this* solar system, *this* sun, *these* forces, it passes through the various spheres—leading first into that central force . . . known as Arcturus—nearer the Pleiades . . . on and *on*—through the *eons* of time . . . or space . . . even passing into the inner forces, *inner* sense, may they again—after a period of nearly ten *thousand* years . . . enter into the earth to make manifest those forces gained in *its* passage. In entering it [the entity] takes on those forms that may be known in the dimensions of that plane which it occupies, there being not only three dimensions—as of the earth—but there may be as seven, in Mercury—or four, in Venus—or five, as in Jupiter. There may be only one as Mars. There may be many more as in those of Neptune, or they may become even as nil—until purified in Saturn's fires.

Reading 5749-14

(Q) *Can oneness be attained . . . on any system, or must it be in a particular one?*

(A) Depending upon what system the entity has entered, to be sure. It may be completed in any of the many systems.

(Q) *Must the solar cycle be finished on earth, or can it be completed on another planet, or does each planet have a cycle of its own which must be finished?*

(A) If it is begun on the earth it must be finished on the earth. The solar system of which the earth is a part is only a portion of the whole. For, as indicated in the number of planets about the earth, they are of one and the same—and they are relative one to another. It is the cycle of the whole system that is finished, see?

Reading 311-2

The common . . . theory that incarnation into the earth plane is the only source of incarnation or appearance is erroneous, you see . . . when . . . a soul—enters in . . . *this* . . . *present* solar system's forces, the contacts or the relative relationships bear out the cycles of appearances in the various spheres of development; as in Mercury—the *mental* life, its relative position to . . . *this* solar system's center, making for those radiations in those forms . . . which represents *mental* in its greater aspect. Then, as in Venus . . . [the development is] more in the form of *love*. In Mars and its radial effect or position about the solar center . . . make for those . . .

known as vengeance, wrath, madness, and such; and can one but know that each thought, each act, is that being builded . . . As in earth—we have that position in which matter takes all its various forms of presentation of a given energy, *or* force, as radiated from the various effects of this solar aspect, and take on *bodily* form, occupying a position of, as it were, three in one—or all force in *this* sphere taking on that appearance of that known as threefold . . . As in Jupiter—taking on those ennobling forces, whether they be from earth, from Venus, from Mercury, from Mars, they are *broadened*, they are *changed* in their aspects, in their forms, as they are taken on in and about *this* sphere. As in Saturn—that to whom all insufficient matter is cast for its remoulding , its changing into the various spheres of its activity, either re-entering through those of the Uranian—which makes for the accentuations of very good or very bad, and making . . . for *extraordinary* conditions . . .

Reading 2794-3

As has been indicated by some, ye are part and parcel of a universal consciousness or God—and thus all that is within the universal consciousness, or the universal awareness; as the stars, the planets, the sun, the moon. Do ye rule them or they rule thee? They were made for thy own use, as an individual—yea, that is the part [they play], the thought thy Maker, thy Father-God thinks of thee. For ye are as a corpuscle in the body of God; thus a co-creator with Him, in what ye think, in what ye do.

Reading 5757-1

When the heavens and the earth came into being, this meant the universe as the inhabitants of the earth know same; yet there are many suns in the universe—those even about which our sun, our earth, revolve; and all are moving toward some place—yet space and time appear to be incomplete.

Then time and space are but one. Yet the sun, that is the center of this particular solar system, is the center; and, as has been . . . known of old, it [the sun] is that about which the earth and its companion planets circulate, or evolve [revolve?].

The beginnings of the understanding of these [facts], and their influ-

ences upon the lives of individuals, were either thought out, evolved or
interpreted by those of old, without the means of observing same as
considered today necessary in order to understand.

Astronomy is considered a science and astrology as foolishness. Who
is correct? One [astrology] holds that because of the position of the
earth, the sun, the planets, they are balanced one with another in some
manner, some form; yet that they have nothing to do with man's life or
the expanse of life, or the emotions of the physical being in the earth.

Then, why and how do the effects of the sun *so* influence other life in
the earth and not affect *man's* life, man's emotions?

As the sun has been set as the ruler of this solar system, does it not
appear to be reasonable that it *has* an effect upon the inhabitants of the
earth, as well as upon plant and mineral life in the earth . . .

Thus as we find given, the sun and the moon and the stars were
made also—this being the attempt of the writer to convey to the individual the realization that there *is* an influence in their activity! For,
remember, they—the sun, the moon, the planets—have their marching
orders from the divine, and they move in same. [Genesis 1:14: "And God
said, Let there be lights in the firmament of heaven to divide the day
from the night; and let them be for signs . . . "]

Man alone is given that birthright of free will. He alone may defy his
God!

Reading 5755-2

. . . souls projected themselves into matter [earth], and thus brought
that conscious awareness of themselves entertaining the ability of creating without those forces of the spirit of truth.

Reading 5755-1

Hence we find how, as ye draw your patterns from these [the sun and
planets], that they become a part of the whole [individual or solar-
whole]. For ye are *relatively* related to all that ye have contacted in materiality [the earth], mentality, spirituality! All of these are a portion of
thyself in the material plane.

In taking form [material] they become a mental body with its
longings for its home, with right and righteousness [heaven].

Then that ye know as thy mental self is the form taken, with all of its variations as combined from the things it has been [has experienced] within, without, and in relationship to the activities in materiality as well as in the spheres or various consciousness . . .

Reading 1297-1

As in the studies of the entity it is seen that the soul of man is a mere speck in space, yet the soul . . . is that vital force or activity which is everlasting. Though the earth, though the stars, may pass away; though there may be changes in the universe as to the relative position, these are brought about by those combinations of that speck of human activity as relative *to* the soul's expression in any sphere of experience.

Reading 3744-4

(Q) Is it proper for us to study the effects of the planets on our lives in order to better understand our tendencies and inclinations, as influenced by the planets?

(A) When studied aright, [it is] very, very, very much so. How aright then? In that influence as is seen in the influence of the knowledge already obtained by mortal man. Give more of that into the lives, giving the understanding *that the will must be the ever guiding factor to lead man on, ever upward.*

Reading 1347-1

The earth is the Lord's and the fullness thereof. The universe He called into being for purposes that the individual soul, that might be one with Him, would have . . . those influences for bringing this to pass or to be in the experience of every soul. For hath it not been given that the Lord thy God hath not willed that any soul should perish? but He hath prepared with every temptation a means, a way of escape. Hence . . . the period of the entrance [birth] is not ruled by the position [of sun and planets] but it may be judged by the position as to the influence . . . upon an entity's experience because of the entity's application of self's abilities relative to its position in the universal scheme of things . . .

Reading 254-21

(Q) What is a horoscope reading?

(A) That in which the planets and their relative forces [here] having to do with the planets that, control the actions without respect of will or without respect of the earthly existences through which the body has passed.

(Q) *Do horoscope readings include former appearances in the earth plane?*

(A) Not at all. The former appearances and the relation of the solar forces in the Universe have their relations to what might be termed life readings . . . [while an astrology chart indicates] the science of the solar system and its relation to various phases of earth's existence [as it] may mean for anyone. In life existence in earth's plane, and the entity's relation to other sphere [as in a life reading] a different condition, for the sojourn in other spheres than earth's plane controls more the conditions or the *urge* of the individual, just as we see . . . an individual controlled by the surroundings, or by the circumstances . . . yet the urge, the latent forces . . . [of] two individuals raised under the same environment, of the same blood, would have different urges. These received from experiences the spirit entity gains in other spheres, correlated with that of its present circumstance . . . for . . . a horoscope is only the mathematical calculation of earth's position in the Universe at any given time, while in the life reading would be the correlation of the individual with a given time and place, with its relative force as applied and received through other spheres and manifested in earth's sphere in the flesh, and the development being the extenuation of the soul's development manifested in the earth plane . . .

Reading 5755-2

. . . though there may be worlds, many universes, even much as to solar systems, greater than our own that we enjoy in the present, this earthly experience on this earth is a mere speck when considered even with our own solar system. Yet the soul of man, thy soul, encompasses *all* in this solar system or in others . . .

But hast thou conceived—or canst thou conceive—the requirements of the influence to meet all the idiosyncrasies of a *single* soul? How many systems would it require? In thyself we find oft one friend for this, another for that, another for this relationship, another for the prop, another to arouse. Yet all are the work of His hand, are thine to possess, thine to use . . .

Is God's hand short, that there would not be all that each soul would require?

Reading 4035-1

For the entity finds itself a body, a mind, a soul—three; or the earth consciousness as a three-dimensional plane in one.

So man's concept of the Godhead is three-dimensional—Father, Son and Holy Spirit. The communication or the activity or the motivating force we find is three-dimensional—time, space and patience. Neither of these exists in fact, except in the concept of the individual as it may apply to time or space or patience.

Reading 633-2

Just as the entity's attending this or that university . . . would make for a parlance peculiar unto itself. Even though individuals may study the same line of thought, one attending Harvard, another Yale, another Oxford, another Stanford, another the University of Arizona, they each would carry with them the vibrations created by their very activity in those environs.

In the same way emotions arise from . . . activity in a particular sojourn, and are called the *spirit* of the institution to which the entity may have carried itself . . .

So we find those astrological sojourns making these vibrations or impressions in the present entity . . .

Reading 2823-1

Then there are the sojourns in other realms of the solar system which represent certain attributes. Not that ye maintain a physical earth-body in Mercury, Venus, Jupiter, Uranus or Saturn; but there is an awareness or a consciousness in those realms when absent from the body, and the response to the position those planets occupy in this solar system . . .

Thus ye oft find in thy experiences that places, peoples, things and conditions are a part of self as if ye were in the consciousness of same.

Each entity is a part of the universal whole. All knowledge, all understanding that has been a part of the entity's consciousness, then, is a part of the entity's experience.

Thus the unfoldment in the present is merely becoming aware of that experience through which the entity, either in body or in mind—has passed in a consciousness.

2

●

The Akashic Record or Book of Life

Editor's Note: Here is how Edgar Cayce described his inner journey to get information and how it appeared to him during one of his psychic readings.

Reading 294-19

I see myself as a tiny dot out of my physical body, which lies inert before me. I find myself oppressed by darkness and there is a feeling of terrific loneliness. Suddenly, I am conscious of a white beam of light. As this tiny dot, I move upward following the light, knowing that I must follow it or be lost.

As I move along this path of light I gradually become conscious of various levels upon which there is movement. Upon the first levels there are vague, horrible shapes, grotesque forms such as one sees in nightmares. Passing on, there begin to appear on either side misshapen forms of human beings with some part of the body magnified. Again there is change and I become conscious of gray-hooded forms moving downward. Gradually, these become lighter in color. Then the direction changes and these forms move upward and the color of the robes grows rapidly lighter. Next, there begin to appear on either side vague outlines of houses, walls, trees, etc., but everything is motionless. As I pass on, there is more light and movement in what appear to be normal cities and towns. With the growth of movement I become conscious of sounds, at first indistinct rumblings, then music, laughter, and singing of birds. There is more and more light, the colors become very beautiful, and there is the sound of wonderful music. The houses are left behind, ahead there is only a blending of sound and color. Quite suddenly, I come upon a hall of records. It is a hall without walls, without ceiling, but I am conscious of seeing an old man who hands me a large book, a record of the individual for whom I seek information.

Editor's Note: The Cayce readings make it quite clear that each soul is constantly adding to his or her record, whether in the dimensions of Earth or in planetary dimensions. A typical reading began as this next one.

Reading 1990-3

Yes, we have the entity here, and those records that are a part of the entity's experience through the earth's plane, as well as through those interims of sojourn in the environs about the earth . . .

Editor's Note: The akasha is not necessarily a total record of the individual's deeds mixed in with the whole of humanity, although a nation, as an entity, might have its own record. In fact, the Cayce readings indicate that this is true. The individual's soul record is one's own and like no other.

Reading 1292-1

Each soul, each body, each individual, is an individual entity; and that done, that thought, becomes as a living record of the experience of that individual entity . . . in whatever sphere of consciousness this activity may be and is recorded upon the skein of time and space.

Reading 566-1

In giving, then, the astrological influences, these would vary considerably from that as would be seen from the spiritual—or the . . . soul experience in the earth's plane. Were this entity's experiences given from the purely astrological science, as accepted in many quarters, these would vary entirely from this [record] which may be given here, or that is viewed from here—for these are the Akashian records of the entity's or soul's development. As to how the present experience, with its environs, will be acted or influenced . . . will have little influence from the astrological standpoint. The entity will be governed rather by the reaction of the experience in the earth's plane through its appearances, rather than astrological influences.

Reading 2571-1

Thus in giving the interpretations of the records here, we would give not only the environmental but also the hereditary influences; not merely from the material lineage but from the mental and spiritual. For these, too, are a part of the heritage of each and every soul.

While there are those influences [from the planets], those urges latent and manifested, know that no urge surpasses the will of the entity—that birthright given each soul that it may know itself to be itself and by choice become one with the Creator . . .

For, each soul . . . *is* a co-creator with the universal consciousness; making those activities for self, for others . . .

For, the astrological sojourns represent the mental or dream forces; while the material earthly sojourns represent the expression through the emotions—or the reaction . . . in expression, in experiences that may be had, may be sought, may be shunned by the entity.

Reading 1401-1

It should be understood that the earthly sojourn [incarnations] urges are [pertained] to the emotions, while the mental or innate urges are from the experiences of the soul in the environs about the earth.

But these are merely urges or inclinations, not impelling forces, and these used in their proper relationships as warnings, or as those things to embrace, may be applied in the experience for helpful forces and influences.

Know, however, that . . . what the will does about that which is set as its ideal in a mental, in a material or in the . . . spiritual [experiences]—and then having the courage to carry out that ideal—makes the difference between the constructive and creative . . . relationships and those that make one become rather as a drifter or a ne'er-do-well, or one very unstable and unhappy.

Reading 1235–1

For Life is a continuous experience. And the mind, the soul, the will, are those influences that act through the material manifestation for the improvement, the development, or for the retardment to the whole of the experience.

For each soul enters each experience for a development, that it may be prepared to dwell with that it seeks as its goal.

Hence the necessity of each entity . . . setting its ideal in each experience.

Hence we find in the developments through those activities of an entity in a material sojourn or through an astrological experience are but the evolution, or making practical. For it is not what an individual or an entity may proclaim that counts, but what each soul . . . does about that it has set as its ideal in relationships to . . . [other] individuals about same.

Reading 5366–1

Yet may this entity be set apart. For through its experiences in the earth, it has advanced from a low degree to that which may not even necessitate a reincarnation in the earth. Not that it has reached perfection but there are realms for instruction if the entity will hold to that ideal . . .

Remember, there are material urges [here] and there are materials in other consciousnesses not three–dimensions alone.

Reading 1796–1

Thus we find this entity—as each entity— is in the present the result of that the entity has applied of Creative influences . . . in every phase of its experience. Thus it makes for that called by some karma, by others racial hereditary forces . . .

And . . . [which] (as are accepted) are in their reality the activities of the *mind* of the entity in its choices through the experiences in the material, in the mental, in the spiritual planes.

Emotions and the Glandular Centers

Reading 2620-2

Thus, as we find in this entity, they [the planets] give expression in the abilities, which find manifestation in the material body through developments or attunements in the glandular system of the body *for* material expression.

Thus upon the skein of time and space is the record of each soul made. In patience, in persistence may such be read . . .

As to the appearances or sojourns in the earth—these we find expressed or manifested in the material body through the senses. Do understand, do interpret the difference between the emotions that arise from the sensory system and those that arise from the *glandular* system alone. True, physically these interchange; yet one [the glandular] represents the *whole* of the development, the other [sensory] represents the step by step activity by an entity in its activity through the material world.

Reading 263-13

The spiritual contact is through the glandular forces of creative energies . . .

Thus we find the connection, the association of the spiritual being with the mental self, at those centers [glandular] from which the reflexes react to all of the organs, all of the emotions, all of the activities of a physical body.

Editor's Note: In the 281 series of Cayce's discourses, each of the seven glands, or psychic centers, is said to be attuned or related to a planet, as follows:

Pituitary: Jupiter (third-eye chakra)
Pineal: Mercury (crown chakra)
Thyroid: Uranus (throat chakra)
Thymus: Venus (heart chakra)
Adrenals: Mars (solar plexus chakra)
Lyden: Neptune (navel chakra)
Gonads: Saturn (root chakra).

3

●

Free Will vs. Stellar and Planetary Influence

Reading 5-2

These [astrological] influences are not greater than the will of the entity. While the varied aspects may be said to *rule* the entity, yet the *entity*—as everyone—should rather, with its own will, *rule* those integral aspects in the affairs—of the stars, as well as of self's own life. Rather . . . than the stars *ruling* the life, the life should rule the stars—for man was created a little bit higher than all the rest of the whole universe, and is capable of harnessing, directing, enforcing, the laws of the universe.

Reading 311-3

In *any* influence, will—a self, the ego, the I Am—is the greater force *to* be dealt with, but as numbers do influence, as astronomical and astrological conditions do influence, a *knowledge* of same certainly gives an individual a foresight into relationships with individuals.

Reading 3340-1

Astrological aspects may or may not become a part of the experience physically for the entity. For these are merely urges, and the will—that which designates God's creation of man from the rest of the animal world—rules as to what an individual soul does with opportunities in relationships with the fellow man.

Reading 1646–2

For, will is that factor . . . which gives the ability to choose that as may be for the development or the retardment. For, as has so oft been indicated, there is today—now—set before each and every entity, every soul, that which is life and death, good and evil. Each entity, each soul, chooses in its manifestations.

Reading 815–6

Not that there are not definite helps to be attained from astrology, but those who live by same the more oft are controlled rather than controlling their own lives and their destinies.

Astrology is a fact, in most instances. But astrological aspects are but signs, symbols. *No influence* is of greater value or of greater help than the *will* of an individual. Use such directions [from the planets] as stepping-stones. Do not let them become stumbling-stones in thy experience.

Reading 1719–1

. . . *will*, that factor which may be trained, even as the mental forces, and *will*, that developer in the material force, being the balance between influences . . . innately built or those of that karmic influence that makes for the *freedom* of the mental being; for in Truth one finds freedom, for he that findeth the Truth is free indeed.

Reading 630–2

. . . it is not so much that an entity is influenced because the Moon is in Aquarius or the Sun in Capricorn or Venus or Mercury in that or the other house, sign, or the Moon and Sun sign, in that one of the planets is in this or that position in the heavens; but rather because those positions in the heavens are from the *entity* having been in that sojourn as a soul! This is how the planets have the greater influence in the earth upon the entity, see? For the application of an experience is that which makes for the development of a body, a mind, *or* a soul. For, how has it been written? "He that knows to do good and doesn't, to him it is sin." Then, the altering or changing factor in an influence is the application of the *will*, that which makes a soul, an entity—that dwells in that called man or woman (means the same)—capable, through this gift of the Creator, of being one with the Giver.

Reading 441-1

The astrological aspects would vary considerably from that outlined from the position of the planets at the time of birth, or from the causes of the influences that are active in the earth. For, these vary as we find—because of the sojourn of the entity in the environs to which the entity merited or chose its activity from an earthly sojourn. For, as long as an entity is within the confines of that termed the earth's and the sons of the earth's solar system, the developments are within the sojourns of the entity from sphere to sphere; and when completed it begins—throughout the music of the spheres with Arcturus, Polaris, and through those sojourns in the outer sphere.

Reading 451-2

In those experiences, then, as come from the influences of the astrological experience of life, as to how the individual *applies* these *in* their experience makes for that as must be called *true* environ of the entity. As for that which *has* been done in earth, or in *other* experiences in the earth, may be called true heredity. In that which is to be met through experiences in the earth, and that which brings about the changes in the application of that known and felt and *understood* in the experience of an entity in the present as karma, as cosmic influence, as the moving of the spirit forces in an individual's application of its knowledge and understanding of things and conditions—these also are as the use that the entity has made, does make, of *its* ideal. Not ideas, not wishes, not *just* desires—for of the *abundance* of the heart the mouth speaketh! of the *desires* of the soul is effort made! The flesh is often weak, the spirit is *ever* willing!

Reading 452-6

(Q) *What months and years will be of greatest progress for body materially and spiritually?*

(A) These, as indicated and as given, are *builded*; rather than their *influencing* the conditions that come about for changes for material or mental, or spiritual advancement; and are much in the same category as numerological conditions or astrological influences. These influence by the activities that an individual has accomplished in certain periods, that with their cycles bring those influences that act as a stimuli during certain periods.

Reading 457-9

(Q) Should the astrological influences lead us to choose one month or another?

(A) Not necessarily; for, remember—as has been the ideal—all spirit comes from the one source. And as has been indicated, there is that giving of same from the one spirit. Thus the preparation of body and mind, and then offering self as the channel, would insure, would bring about that association that is giving the mother the opportunity for the expressing of the hopes and the desires—and the preparation of same for that channel.

Reading 311-10

(Q) Would it be well for me to make a study of astrology?

(A) Well for everyone to make a study of astrology! for, as indicated, while many individuals have set about to prove the astrological aspects and astrological survey enable one to determine future as well as the past conditions, these are well to the point where the individual understands that these act upon individuals because of their sojourn or correlation of their associations with the environs through which these are shown—see? Rather than the star directing the life, the life of the individual directs the courses of the stars, see?

Reading 262-94

As has been declaimed by a teacher, there is one Glory of the sun, another of the moon, another of the stars; each differing in their Glory according to the purpose for which they each have been established. For what? That man might in himself see the Glory of the Father being made manifest by they each performing their purpose in *their* cooperation, in *their* activity, before Him.

So, in thine own life, in thine own relation, in thine own associations one with another, how speakest *thou*—how readest thou? that ye do this or that in order that ye may be well thought of? or are ye fearful of what another will say because thou art called to do this or that?

Does the sun fear the Glory of the moon, or the moon the sun?

Do the stars fail to shine because the sun is in *His* Glory?

Yea, these should be to each of us that example, even as He gave, "Abide in me, I in thee, and ye shall have and know the Glory of the Father."

Reading 288-50

As the sun, the moon, the stars would be given for signs, for seasons, for days, for years in man's experience—then it would not be amiss that these would indicate the symbols as they were represented in those stages or phases of experience in the earth.

Reading 2608-1

Thus a soul is in the earth, in the material manifestations, as in a school of experience. For, no soul gains knowledge or understanding save through experience.

The experience is not of another's making, but of thine own. For in spiritual truths, His spirit beareth witness with thy spirit—not thy uncle nor thy aunt, nor thy father or mother, but thy soul self.

For, until the Creative Force—or God—becomes a personal experience of the soul it has only been heard of, and the activity more oft is because of what others will say. This may be truly called environment, while those experiences while absent from the body are in that realm in which the soul is present with what it has done about the opportunities in the material plane. Thus this may be truly called a spiritual-hereditary influence. Here it is called astrological aspects.

For ye live, ye move in an environ of dimensions according to the awareness and application of thyself to these influences in thy activity. It is not then what ye think or what ye say that counts, but what thy soul desires, what thy soul hopes for, what thy soul manifests in thy relationships to these environs; that are opportunities for the application of that understanding ye *may* have at any given period of manifestation.

Thus, astrologically, in the solar system of which the earth is a part, other environs are manifestations of the influence that controls centers in the human body—as the brain, the sun—sex, the moon—as the centers through which activity manifests in the five senses of the body, and the centers that manifest same.

To such has been accredited, then, those influences represented in what a soul-entity may have applied in the individual self. *That* magnified, to be absent from the body is to be present with that ye have magnified, or glorified, in thy relationships one with another.

For He hast not willed that a soul should perish, but hath with every temptation prepared a way, a means for correction; and it is through those awarenesses, or those dimensions, that these take their course with an individual entity.

In thyself ye find Venus, Mercury, Mars, Jupiter and Uranus as thy experiences; to be sure with their correlating from earth's experience in the sun *and* the moon.

Either or any of these may be magnified to the detriment of another. It is best that they be correlated, co-balanced. For, as the earth—we find body, mind, soul; in the Godhead we find Father, Son, Holy, Spirit. These are one.

So, in thy dealings, be not the extremist—as may be magnified either from the Uranian or the Venus influence. For these partake of those influences. These cause the urges by their expression, not because of thy being born at any given hour when this or that planet was in the ascendancy, or in the 1st, 2nd or 9th house, but because of thy doings *through* those environs or those dimensions.

In Venus we find the love influence, the desire for beauty.

From Jupiter we find the universality.

In Mercury we find the judgement.

4

•

Planetary Influences

Reading 254-2

(Q) Do the planets have anything to do with the ruling of the destiny of men? If so, what? and what do they have to do with this body?

(A) They do. In the beginning, as our own planet, Earth, was set in motion, the placing of other planets began the ruling of the destiny of all matter as created, just as the division of waters was and is ruled by the moon in its path about the Earth; just so as in the higher creation, as it began, is ruled by the action of the planets about the earth.

The strongest power in the destiny of man is the Sun, first; then the closer planets, or those that are coming in ascendency at the time of the birth of the individual; but let it be understood here, no action of any planet or any of the phases of the Sun, Moon, or any of the heavenly bodies surpass the rule of Man's individual will power—the power given by the Creator of man in the beginning, when he became a living soul, with the power of choosing for himself.

The inclination of man is ruled by the planets under which he is born. In this far the destiny of man lies within the sphere or scope of the planets. With the given position of the Solar system at the time of the birth of an individual, it can be worked out—that is, the inclinations and actions without the will power taken into consideration.

As in this body here [Edgar Cayce] born March 18,1877, three minutes past three o'clock, with the Sun descending, on the wane, the Moon in the opposite side of the Earth (old moon), Uranus at its zenith, hence the body is ultra in its actions. Neptune closest in conjunction, or Neptune as it is termed in Astrological survey, in the ninth house; Jupiter, the higher force of all the planets, save the Sun, in descendency, Venus just coming to horizon, Mars just set, Saturn—to whom all insufficient matter is cast at its decay—opposite the face of the Moon. Hence the inclination as the body is controlled by the Astrological survey at the time of the birth of this body, either (no middle ground for this body) very good or very bad, very religious or very wicked, very rich or always losing, very much in love or hate, very much given to good works or always doing wrong, governed entirely by the will of the body. Will is the educational factor of the body; thence the patience, the persistence, the ever-faithful attention that should be given to the child when it is young.

Reading 398-2

Yes, we have the body, [398], and those conditions in the astrological aspects; especially in reference to those adverse influences that appear eminent in the experience of the entity in the near future; as well as that which has been built by the entity in its sojourns through the spheres of activity where there is such a gathering of influences as to become active in a body-entity.

In giving that which may be understandable, and that which may be helpful from the material angle at this time, as we find, it would be well that all consider the varying aspects from that considered an astrological influence. As we have given through these channels, astrological influences are effective in the experience of each and every entity. However, when the activities of a soul-entity have been such as to cause or to form the appearance of the entity in a particular sphere of activity, the position of the sojourn of the entity *to* the earth *has* the greater influence than just the adverse or benevolent positions of the planet or of a whole solar system upon the *entity's* activity!

Is this understood? [Pause] You should answer! [Mrs. Cayce: I don't quite understand.]

[Mr. Cayce continuing] Then, it is as this: When the activities of an entity, a soul in the earth, have been such that its passage from the earth would become a birth into the realm of matter known as Mars, Venus, Jupiter, Uranus, Neptune, Moon, Mercury, Polaris, or any of these that are effective in the universal influence, you see, the sojourn there *and* the position of the planets *are* more effective than the influence brought to bear because of a position in a certain place or portion of the universal forces, see?

Hence, as we find, these conditions are only as urges; or, as may be termed from some reasons or seasons of thought, the planetary influences from their positions are either benevolent, adverse or inter-between these activities—one drawing upon another; but the entity's *sojourn in* those environs makes the impulse for the mental activity, rather than the *position* of these!

Reading 439-1

So, the astrological sojourns are rather as intuitional influences felt when in meditation or distress in mind, that brings the harking of a something that may be found through the application of self respecting the knowledge self has concerning the Creative Forces in a material world.

Reading 518-1

From the astrological aspects much may be gathered that will be helpful in the entity's experience in the present sojourn. While the astrological aspects make for general tendencies in many entities' experience, the planetary sojourn in the earth's environ deals more with the mental development of an entity than just because the stars, the sun, the moon or any of the zodiacal signs are in the aspects at the hour or period of beginnings in this experience.

Rather has that which has been builded in the soul of the entity brought about its influence, and so does the entity become influenced according to its activities in relationships to that which has been the understanding or comprehension of the universal laws, as it—the entity—is related to same. For, without knowledge there is not the comprehension; and without understanding it does not become practical in the material development or manifestation of a soul.

Reading 528–14

Hence the astrological influences are more to the spiritual or *innate* urges, that are aroused by the deeper meditating of the mental self.

Reading 541–1

In giving that which may be helpful to this entity through such information, it would be well to include something as to how this is obtained; that there may be some credence given, and at least an attempt on the part of the entity to apply and to verify things that may be said and given –which will be as some experiences that have been in the entity's life; and then that as to what the entity and body in the present may do *about* that it knows of itself and its abilities in the present.

As each soul enters in the earth, there are purposes other than that which may be arising from desire of those that physically are responsible for such an advent.

For, the soul seeks from the realm of spirituality to give expression of that it as an entity or soul may do with its experiences in the mental realm, as well as about that it *has* done in a physical realm.

Hence the law that is ever present; like attracts like; like begets like. Hence there is the attraction as from the desires of those in the physical calling to the sources of generation in the flesh, to the sources of creation or of spirit in the spiritual realm.

Hence there is often a real purpose in the soul, as in this soul, seeking a period of expression of self; and finding it in that about the bodies when there is the period of presentation. For, while the physical begins at conception, the spiritual and mental is as the first breath taken into the physical—that becomes then a living soul, with a physical organism for manifestation during the sojourn in that particular experience.

Then, what influences such a journey, such an advent of the soul from the unseen into materiality? Development of the soul that it may take its place, through the lessons gained in physical experience, in those classes or realms of soul activity in an infinite world—among those that have passed in their activity through the various realms; seeking then (as that which first called every soul and body into experience) that of companionship. Hence we have as much hereditary and environmental forces in soul's experience (or the developed soul to such an experience) as we have in the law of the earth, as to that which is hereditary from the parentage of a body—and the environs of the body, as to what is the trend of thought.

Reading 553-1

In coming into an experience such as this entity and soul did on the 27th of June, 1900, in Centerville, Michigan, was this by accident—or was the soul from another realm or plane seeking for expression that it, the soul, might build or renew self in specific directions for that purpose for which it has come into experience or consciousness in materiality?

Then, it behooves all that there should be as great consideration given as to where the soul came from as to where the soul is going!

For, as in thine own experiences in the material things, if the composition or nature of wood, stone, or plaster even, is given to the builder (as in self), it is known by the experience as to what it (the material, as the soul) will do in response to certain conditions in its experience as a useful material in a given line. It is known how much exposure it may bear, how much textile strength in its various usages or environs it will meet, and what necessary elements are required as a stimuli in coating, mixing or the like, to aid it to be a better material.

So the soul in its activity, if it is known from what environ it has received its training—as in mental impulses—or what are the environs through its earthly sojourns, it may be seen or known as to what may be the necessary influences to make for better preparations in the present.

That the systems in the earth's environ or earth's orbit are places or conditions or spheres of abode for those particular classified environs of a soul, is not only reasonable but a practical thing—if properly considered.

Hence we find some variation as to what has been considered a source of information respecting influences in the affairs of human endeavor.

That the soul may have sojourned in an experience in Mercury, Jupiter, Saturn, Uranus, or any of those sister planets of the Sun in this particular environ, makes for a nature in the mental capacities and abilities of a soul.

So that when there is (as has been proclaimed) a bombardment, as it were, of the planetary influence upon any other realm by its proximity of the relative position—or by the influence in the realm of etheronic energies that affect the activity, these influence the soul–mind much in the manner as an earthly training in any particular division of human or commercial endeavor trains a mind, a body, to meet emergencies in the experience of the body–associations with conditions in the human experience.

Reading 555–1
As to the sojourns in the environs of the earth known as the astrological influences through the entity or soul sojourn in those environs, they come as habits or experiences might by living in such an environ in an earth's experience that influences the aptitude or activity of a soul. But ever as the balance, as the safety, as the governor for each soul stands He that has given, "In my Father's house are many mansions; if it were not so, I would have told you. I go to prepare a place for you; that where I am, there ye may be also." If the soul then makes those preparations in the activities in any sojourn, or in the varied experiences with the relationships it may have with its fellow man, the preparation then comes for that sojourn, that experience, that home, where the sojourns of earth, the turmoils and strife of the experiences in any material relationships may be—not forgotten, but used in such ways and manners as to bring to that soul the awareness which He has promised: "I will bring to you remembrance of those things from the beginning, that where I am there ye may be also."

Reading 566–1
As there was in the entering of the entity's inner forces into this physical body, the first will come at the age of seven, at fourteen, at twenty-two—these will be decided changes, or one will so lap over the other—but may be said to be periods when changes will come to this entity; for there was some lapse of time (as time is counted from the material) between the physical birth and the spiritual birth.

Reading 585–2

. . . Do not confuse the sojourns in the astrological with material things, for they are mental urges—yet acted upon from material things may oft bring confusion.

Reading 688–2

The astrological influences also have their place in the inner urges that are latent and awakened, through the application of self as respecting will and opportunity in relationships of that which is the motivative force in every mental process in the soul's activity. For with the purpose, with the desire, ever does there come—as has ever been seen—the opportunity, the experience, for what the soul does about that it has gained in its sojourn through *whatever* realm of consciousness it has passed or is passing. That which remains as being unaware in the consciousness of an individual entity remains as the mysteries or the hidden influences.

SELECTED CASE STUDIES

Reading 122–1

Mrs. Cayce: You will give a horoscope reading for this entity, a reading giving the effects of the solar systems on the life and destiny of this entity in the present earth plane, naming the planet, or position, from which the soul took its last flight. You will give the vocation in life for which this body is best adapted, or may adapt itself, giving also the high points of the life in former appearances, giving the name and place of sojourn in the earth plane, with the characteristics as brought forward in its personality in the present life.

Mr. Cayce: Yes, we have the entity as here, December 29, 1876. In this we find the present entity completed in the afternoon, two fifty-eight, and in the present sphere we find the position taken from that of Venus, with the help of those influences from Mercury, Mars, Saturn and Uranus at times, with the assistance of Jupiter; afflictions coming in Moon's effect and in Sagittarius. Hence we have an individual, without respect will's manifestation in the present earth's plane, of exceptional abilities, and of many contradictory manifestations of the effects of planets, or of astrological conditions as has been considered and studied by peoples for many ages; yet, with that influence as will be seen through the correct interpretation of astrological effect in earth's development that would be manifest in the present entity, and the views as are held on life in earth plane, and the body's precept and concept of life and its effect, and the transmutation through the earthly sphere.

Then, without respect of the will, we have one given to be very much attracted to many peoples, of many climes, of many conditions, of many positions, of many phase of many actions. Hence the ability of the entity, when the influences of Mercury, especially, are considered, to gain much by what has been and is termed in physical plane as actual experience, and many learn *only* from such.

[This is] An entity that would be, and is, a wonderful study from the psychological and pathological viewpoint of the development in the mental and spiritual spheres, as manifest in the physical plane.

One given to study, read, much of other conditions, other positions, other experiences, of those in many spheres, especially those of royalty and their physical action in material world.

One that would be given to the study of anatomical or anatomic conditions, that have to do with the elements as of Venus persuasion.

In the elements, then, of that wherein the mental development, the spiritual environment through which the entity has passed in other spheres:

One who could have made a wonderful success in that as of the metaphysical physician.

One who may at present make a success in the study of those elements pertaining to vibration and the rejuvenation of physical forces in human anatomy, that may be revived by elements (physical) of vibration.

In the development, we have many phases through which entity has passed in earth's plane, coming in contact with many of the elements of purely physical carnal plane, in contact with many of the mental and spiritual and soul plane. The entity may develop, yet, far in those forces pertaining to the occult forces, for with the present development in the earth's plane, and with the renewed elements as are manifest in earth's plane, through influence of Uranian forces in earth's plane, in the next

six to thirteen months the entity may gain much of knowledge that will
bring better conditions for self and for others, giving then an understanding that would, will the will but manifest in that manner in assisting others.

Reading 142–1

We have the body and those relations with the universal forces as
are latent in the present entity's sojourn in the earth's plane.

In entering we find the entity comes under the influence of Jupiter
and Mercury with benevolent influences in Uranus and in Venus; hence
we will find there will be many unusual conditions as will surround
those influences as will be exhibited in the life of the entity. Yet as we
find, there is also presented, through those cosmic influences and
through the astrological conditions, those of the warnings as would be
presented for the development of the mental, the physical and the spiritual influences as will become manifested through urges as will be exhibited in this body. Principally these have to do with those conditions
regarding temper and the exercising of same as regards the will's influence. Not, then, that the will of the entity shall be broken but that same
shall be guided in those directions that will bring the more benevolent
and more powerful influence in the life through the Jupiterian influence.

Again we find that there will appear the square of those conditions
between Mars and Uranus with Jupiter in the twelfth year in which the
warning is especially against the relations of the entity as regarding
firearms. For, as will be seen from the appearances in the earth's plane
and those influences as were brought to bear, there will be the necessity
of the correct influence towards same rather than that bringing detrimental influence or misunderstanding of the correct application of self
toward those conditions.

As we find these greater influences are to be the ruling forces in the
development of the entity:

There appears, as we see, the greater influence in Jupiter and in Mercury, with the benevolent influence in Uranus which becomes as exceptional conditions in the urges; being then very decided in the likes
and dislikes, being inclined toward those conditions and positions of

estate and of high mental and physical influence; inclined then toward aspiring to same through the abilities of the mental.

Hence the injunction as is given toward the direction of the will's influence in the life as respecting control of temper. For in this there may be brought those detrimental conditions especially as regarding the misapplication of station or position, rather than inclined towards those not of the plebian but of those in the position of the leader. For the natural intent of the entity is toward that of the natural leader in the mental, in the social, in the political, in the financial forces of those who surround the entity.

Remember, then, in the astrological forces and influence, that the assurance of the elements of the training are in the first twelve years of the present experience in this earth's plane . . .

The urge as will be seen in the present experience will be that respecting the religious trend of the entity, and the especial interest in the law as set forth in same, especially as applying to populace . . .

As to the abilities, then, in the present, we find these are to be builded, rather than as exhibited in the present time, through those influences brought to bear upon the urges and the desires as are expressed by light in the field of the study in law and in the financial forces and principles of the land and all other lands . . .

(Q) In the astrological phases it has been given by one from that plane "for we knew this entity before, for he comes from among us." What plane would he come from, or planet? [see 136-59]

(A) Jupiter, for in this as given, there is seen the plane of the just, and of those who present the powers in the earth's sphere.

Reading 143-1

This entity, we find, took its flight, or position, from the planet of Uranus, with Venus and Mercury controlling the destiny in the present earth's plane. Hence the necessity of the entity's training, especially, in those elements having to do with purity in love and affection, and of nobleness and of goodness for the goodness that comes with that mode of expressing itself in earth's plane, for with the entity under these influences, with the exceptional conditions as come from influences of Uranus, we find the entity's manifestations in the present plane will be exceptionally good or very bad.

With these influences, also there should be guarded the physical health of the entity, especially in those conditions that have to do with the throat and tonsils, and with kidney eliminations, for under the square of Mercury, with those of Saturn, and with Venus and Jupiter in the abstruse [obtuse?] condition, or position, would come those conditions to be warned of in physical effects. These, or the first, we will find will occur in March 1925. With some conditions that may arise, this might prove detrimental. Hence the warning for physical conditions. Again will this occur in November 1932.

The elements then, as we find, without respect of the will, and of the training that may be accorded the entity's mental development, which becomes an attribute from the physical to the soul of the entity, these conditions:

One that may love too well but not wisely.

One that may be too indiscreet in person, yet with all good intentions from the entity's viewpoint.

One with the correct training, in these two elements especially, will give much to the world, of forces through the ennobling influences of the life led and known among many peoples.

One that would give much of the understanding through the love and ennobling forces in those mental attributes of soul's manifestations, called psychic or spiritual forces in earth's plane.

One that will find the peculiar adaptability to every condition through which the physical labors may lead the entity.

One that should be trained in those lines, especially, of musical forces in the understanding of same in the lives of individuals who receive the vibrations from same to ennoble their lives, rather than an operator or musician itself.

One whose life would lead to an early matrimonial career, though not wisely, unless correctly directed in its early life.

One who may be given, through the correct training, much of the influences to be shed over many peoples . . .

In the personalities that may be exhibited in the present earth's plane, we find, we *will* find, those of the nature of the love of pomp and of show.

In the next, in that that becomes contradictory to the conditions first shown.

In the next, the desire to be led or directed by others.

We would give, in the summing of the present, that the entity's mental, with consideration of the physical health, be directed in those ennobling influences coming from its sojourn in Jupiter, Venus and Uranus, and we will bring an exceptional and acceptable entity to the world's development.

Reading 169-1

We have the entity here, and those relations with the universe and universal forces, as are latent and exhibited in the present earth's plane.

Now in the development of this entity there are conditions that are worthy of note for those studying that phase of man's development that relates to the akashic record as is made by each individual, as an individual, and the effect same has on continuity of existence as related to earth's experience and of the astrological relations with the earth. For, while these are as urges in the earthly experience, there is ever that factor to be dealt with, or accounted for in man's individuality, that is called *will*; as to how this may shape, mould, or change those various experiences of an entity in its relation to the whole. For, remember, each entity has within itself many spheres that are as capable of advancement as the individual itself; changed according to the application of will *in* material essence to the essence of the whole.

In entering the present sphere and experience we find the entity [169], coming under the influence of Jupiter, Mercury, and of Neptune, with variableness in Uranus and Saturn.

In the urges as latent and exhibited in the present experience, irrespective of will's application [we find the following]:

One ever interested in things pertaining to mystery, and the entity would make an excellent detective.

One that has high ennobling influences in the life as respecting own development and relationships to others. This, as seen, would make a variableness—with the urge as directed towards detective work of the general nature—and hence combative in an influence.

One of high mental abilities, and the ability to express or to make known to others those of the laws as pertain to mental ability and the application of same as pertaining to varied relationships in the material plane.

One that will ever be a student of human nature. Hence in accord with that of the detective, or business, or speaking, or writing. Yet one that may—in an incorrect application *of* the knowledge or judgement concerning same—bring evil influence in the life; for the entity, while headstrong in many respects, is easily led or persuaded when that as presented—for the moment—represents any desire felt (for the moment) without due consideration given to the fruit of that desired.

In the application of these urges from the astrological influence, first we would find the entity with abilities. Then in the application *of* the ability, be guided, directed, in that channel of applying will's forces and the abilities toward that *correct* in the way of developing the self and in directing others in development of their selves; for each has its own peculiar niche or place to fill in the affairs, not only of each household, locality, state or nation, but in the universal forces as applied to the entity's abilities, and that *responsibility* that rests *with* the entity's application of that attained, or to which it may develop or guide others. Then, be sure self is set aright in the knowledge of that which would develop an entity, and be guided aright in application of self thereto; for there is no foundation set save as in Him, that is the way, the life, the light, the water, the vine, and is in Him *through* whom all live, move, and have their being. Then find self and self's relationship to that presented through that life, and govern self and self's relation to others in the light of that applied to self's own experience.

In that of likes—dislikes—and the influences in the present experience:

One with high ideals.

Lover of *clean* sports, of that that brings clean living in the lives of others; yet this in itself, not guided aright, may be made a stumbling block in self's own development; for, remember, each and every individual views conditions from its own development, and to its own being the conditions are as only so far as each has attained . . .

In the abilities of the entity as seen in the present, these would relate particularly to *people* and to things, whether of lands or of study of any nature as pertains to law, land, or peoples—and in *either* of these would the entity make the greater success in the financial ways and manners; yet for the greater development keep first the understanding of self and self's relationship to others first and foremost. Beware of entanglements with those of the opposite sex, especially those whose birthdays come in May. Beware of conditions as pertaining to bodily ills that have to do with the digestive system. Keep self unspotted from low relationships, and keep thyself bodily clean.

Reading 172-3

We have the entity and those relations with the universe and universal forces, as are latent and exhibited in the present entity. The body entered in the earth's plane in this experience in the early hours of the day–five forty-five a.m.

In entering, we find the entity coming under the influence of Mercury, Neptune, Venus, Mars, Jupiter, with those astrological influences of the Moon, with the variations as appear through the application of will as respecting these. Astrologically, many of the innate experiences, and much as has to do with the body as related to same, or groups, would be in keeping with the experiences of the body. As much as has to do with the development of the *mental* forces and the application of self as respecting these, as would become individual in its application, these would *not* conform to those ordinary rules as have been set forth as astrological.

Coming under the influences, then, astrologically, we find: One whose mental capacities and abilities are good, yet ever being weighted by those in Neptune and of Venus finds individual contradiction as related to individuals; that is, individuals often feel the entity—in its application of the mental forces and abilities—is not applying self in directions that are for the best, as others see it; yet, as a leader for a group, or as one that would influence groups or masses, the entity's mental forces far surpass many that are called speakers, writers, teachers, or even exhorters. Hence the entity finds self with a great *many* of the mass influenced by self, and often finds self estranged or at advarience [variance] with many who *should* be the closest friends, yet those that are the closest friends, associates, knowing the body, the personality, the individuality—if you please—better learn to love the entity for its worth to them. Not as eye servants, but as one appreciating, feeling—innately— the influence *of* one with an experience worth while, and one made worth while to many.

Under the influences in Venus and Mars, love for those things as pertain to military affairs—yet peaceful in its attitude; not wholly as a pacifist in extreme, yet rather as one that weighs same with those of the mental and of the application of the psychological influences under such conditions. This bringing changes, then, and has ever—and will yet bring much change to the entity, even in *this* experience; that is, *force* of arms, whether of firearms or of those elements that have to *do with* same.

In Jupiter comes that of the bigness, nobleness, and the broad-mindedness of the entity—and this, varied with the elements as are seen and as has been given, shows how the variations *as* come individually, and to groups and masses.

One, then, that is in the position of meaning much to many.

One loving or desiring changes of scene, and in varied circumstances, knowing and feeling that to experience the influence that changes or alters individuals *and* groups *is* the way for self to *understand* others the better.

One that loves music, and the art of music; as a critic, rather than as applied. As the voice of individuals or of nature, rather than as instrumental, so far as any individual instrument concerned. Rather in groups and masses and their altering in harmony and its changes, for at times harmony is desired by the entity. Then contrasts are necessary for the entity to *understand* conditions that, to the entity, comparisons may be drawn. Hence innately in *every* element, whether in affairs of the heart, or life, of position, of stations in life, there is ever the comparison drawn by the entity. Well, then, that the entity *attain* for self an ideal, rather than mere ideas. Drawing often upon the innate influences in self as related to the mysteries of life, as pertaining to the mysteries of the Beyond—in which the entity often delves, that there may be for the self the greater fullness of the experiences of the entity. To experience, to the entity, is to understand.

Reading 187–1

In the position as is taken in the present plane, we find this comes from Jupiter, with Uranus and Mars, with Saturn and Neptune in the adverse conditions, bringing then to this entity one that will be and is strong of body, and will find, with the proper training, the normal development towards those conditions of the magnanimous, and of those ennobling influences as come in Jupiter; yet with those diverse influences in Uranus will bring very eccentric, very good or very bad, very high tempered, or one that will need the necessity then of being trained in that proper manner, which will give the resources of the urges as are exhibited in the body the opportunity of their development. For with the adverse influence in Mars, that comes with Saturn's conjunction with same, we would bring, under the adverse conditions, when we would have the extremities of the Uranian influence, a force very detrimental to self and others. Hence, as has been given, the necessity, the responsibility, the manner that rests in the hands of those who would guide, guard and direct the trend of the thought of the developing individual.

With the greater influence, we find these will bring many of the ennobling and assisting influences in the earth plane.

One whose abilities will lie in that of the student along the line of monies and of psychological study, either that as the trained mathematician or banker, or as that of the student along psychological and astronomical studies. These may be, however, reversed by the conditions as exhibited and as has been given.

Reading 189–3

In giving the interpretations of those influences in the experience of this entity, these as we find in the astrological and the earthly sojourn make for urges latent and manifested that may be summed up as these—but without respect of will or the applications that have been made in the present experience:

One of high mental capacities, and tending towards the masculine mind; not in manner or mien but in thought; yet patient, persevering, and a latent and manifested tendency towards the arts as well as towards executive abilities; tempered ever with a seeking for the higher, more ennobling influences that are the criterions for a spiritual life.

These we find latent and manifested, and from the astrological and the earthly sojourns we may draw conclusions as to why these are latent and manifested urges in the experience of the entity now called [189].

In the astrological aspects we find Jupiter; Venus in the adverse; Mars in relationships with Jupiter, adverse with Saturn.

Hence little or few changes should be made in the experience of the entity, though—as a matter of fact—many have been made in the present sojourn. Again we may see the influences from the earthly sojourns that activated these influences in the experience of the entity.

Jupiter has made for not only the high ennobling influence but the tendency for relationships that deal with large numbers of peoples.

Being in an adverse position to Venus makes for those innate and manifested forces of the entity making for self a career in the business or associated activities in the experience. Not that there are not latent urges for the home building, but these—as has been indicated—have been rather, and are, from the astrological aspects, adverse rather than benevolent.

The benevolent forces come then rather with the relationships to others, to the groups, to the masses, than with individuals; though the body finds friendships and relationships from under adverse conditions—and oft those adverse influences in the experience of the entity in relationships to individuals—bringing the entity closer to those paternal instincts, those activities for friendships, those activities for long-suffering even in its relationships to individuals or peoples.

In Saturn we find many individual projects, individual activities coming to the experience of the entity. Hence constantly there has been held before the entity oft the prospects which in a material way or in a social or financial way would become more helpful in influence; yet these have often—more often than otherwise—not materialized to their full extent.

Yet as the entity has learned and does learn patience, long-suffering—not in a sense of duty but in a sense of opportunity for soul development—greater has been and will be the peace, the harmony, those influences that will bring the greater soul development.

For these influences are a portion of the experience of every entity entering or passing through the earth's plane.

The earthly sojourns make for rather the innate and manifested urges that come from the emotional forces of the body, while the astrological sojourns make for rather the mental urges.

Reading 195–8

We also have those conditions as have been experienced in the earth plane by the soul and spirit, which complete the present entity, [195], in the present earth plane. We find that the greater influence comes from that of Mercury and Saturn, both being in the birth sign Gemini at the period of birth, but Saturn in that position of the square with Jupiter and Venus. This we find brings many conditions that in the thoughts of others make the appearance of this individual's way of thinking peculiar.

One given to be especially given to the ideas relating to inventions and the development of each that would bring the better conditions to the lives of his fellow man.

One that will find the inclination to be of assistance to many peoples, and will also find many losses, financially, in such conditions, yet building continually in self through such transactions, if the body will but will itself to build upon such conditions.

One that through the influence of Saturn, with the conditions in Jupiter and in Venus, finds little in the felicity of domestic relations, yet ever thoughtful, ever kind, especially to children, showing a great love of development of children and of small pets of every character.

One that will only find joy in domestic relations very late in life, and with the one that is far distant from the age and surroundings of the entity at the time.

One given, especially, to enjoy the pleasures of earthly conditions in every manner and form, though one never forsaking the good intent in each and every such relation.

One that finds the pleasure of earthly forces, especially, in the usage of those conditions called questionable, for these influences are the natural tend, causing the body to travel a great deal, and will find that under certain conditions, as in the present year, when the signs are in the birth sign Gemini, the better conditions will come to the body in the cares of the world and in the development of self, and just after having very strong inclinations to doubt those whom he felt that faith and confidence could be placed in.

One with such inclinations needs to use will more to gain the lessons from each condition, for seldom does the entity gain the lesson as others feel that he should, and in this respect many are the doubts in the mind as to the relations with others.

One that will find the greater financial gain come through the development of the conditions as developed from other sources, through the mind and acts of this entity. These are irrespective of the will, and are the inclinations as we find from the planet effects in the body.

One that will do well to use the will's forces to develop much along the psychic lines, for with the position of Uranus and Neptune in the birth sign gives much to the body's understanding in the present plane of those conditions regarding occult and mystic forces in the earth's plane, and much may develop from the study of such relations, if the body would but exercise its will concerning same.

As to the vocation, we would find from this, it should be in many various lines of endeavors, bordering especially on those of developing of the new, or of those things that make the burdens of the human family easier, or of patents; assisting in developing patents of such nature, the body is best adapted.

Reading 195–14

In taking the position in the present earth's plane, we find the entity took the position from Mercury, with Saturn, Jupiter and Uranus in those positions that affect the life. Hence the conditions that are existent, and have been existent in the present earth plane, of the exceptional nature, or of those conditions wherein we find they have gone to the extreme. Just when there seemed every indication and every hope for success, financially, morally, religiously, physically, those conditions did appear that seemed to turn everything topsy-turvy.

As to the relations these have brought and do bring to the body, then, we find:

The influences of the earthly existences, as we shall see, bring the

greater urges, latent and exhibited, in the present earth plane; though
the influence of Jupiter, square with Saturn and Uranus, brings one of
very exceptional nature, eccentric in many ways and manners.

The entity is one, though, far from close marital relations. For we find
it would be late in the present earth plane before the body would come
in contact with that one with whom such relations would be of a satis-
factory nature, and one far from present surroundings, and very much
younger in years in age.

One who will have much of this world's goods to dispose of. One
who follows or considers much the worldly pleasures, but one who
likes or desires to enjoy the same in his own way and manner.

One who holds love of animal life and of children very high in es-
teem in his own self, and he exhibits the same, unintentionally or
unthoughtedly, for it is the natural intent, as we shall see why.

One who finds many in whom he has placed faith or confidence
have shaken that faith. One who, especially when there is the influence
of Saturn's square with the influence of Mercury, brings such conditions
in the life. Yet these, with the use of will force, may be turned to that
way that will prove beneficial to the development of the entity in the
present earth's plane.

One who will have many years in the earth plane, travelling, visiting
many places; and he will seek one day those positions occupied in other
spheres.

One who, with the influences as seen in Uranus, with Jupiter and
Mercury, may gain a world of influence for good from psychic and occult forces and influences of same.

One who, while holding the high relations toward life in manner of
the religious thought, has no secular religious thought entering into the
dictates of the entity's better forces; rather the oriental than the
occidental; rather that as pertains to the universal brotherhood and the
direct relations with the higher forces than any specific creed or law or
line; and these we shall see why.

One who may give much to the world in the development of conditions that have to do with beneficence and beneficial conditions for the
use of man and mankind in their physical development.

One who will find his greatest influence and force in following out the line of development of those things having to do with patents, or development of the same, as may be done through the analytical mind of this individual. And through the same we will find great amounts of moneys coming to the individual, from unexpected places. From places where there has been little, little, thought given as to the development of same will worldly goods come. Use them aright, then, in a way that will build to that closer connection between the divine from within and that which ever calls for the answering of self and self's usage, to give homage to the divine that is within each and every individual.

Reading 846-2

Bright, bright indeed are those surroundings that portend for a great awakening for the entity before this time next season!

In entering the present experience in the earth, through those associations of the entity's activities in the earth, and in the interims sojourn in this solar aspect, we find—for the more perfect understanding:

Know that the sojourning of the entity or soul in those environs about the earth, or of which the earth is a part, makes for those things that *innately* influence the entity in its associations and activities in the present experience, or in any experience. For, as there is seen from association of ideals, of ideas, and their relative relationships with the activities of an entity, it becomes a portion of same—even as a brogue or as a habit, or as an activity that becomes a part of the emotions or motions of a body. This is an illustration. Not that it manifests, save in the *inner* self.

As we find, there are the influences of Mercury, Jupiter, Mars, Saturn and Uranus in the experience of the entity. And soon there enters the experience in those periods at the birthday in the present year when Jupiter, with Venus' sojourn, makes for the greater awakening or greater development in the application of the entity in this earthly sojourn.

One, then (but this is irrespective of what the entity does about the urges), with a high temper; that may make for a great expression or may make for those influences that would become stumbling experiences in the activities of the entity.

From the activities of the Uranian sojourn, the entity is interested in that which makes for the emotions in the experience of peoples; whether they are of the mystic, occult, scientific, or *ordinary* individuals—as would be termed in common parlance. This makes for the eccentricities of the entity in its relationships with individuals. And it depends upon the application of same as to whether these become as stepping-stones for the higher emotions or higher activities, or whether they become as stumbling-stones over which the entity may—in its application of its ideal—become as one tripped upon its own self.

In Jupiter we find the greater vision, the greater abilities in specific fields of activity; not only from that as accomplished by the entity in its activities in the earth (as will be seen) but through the application of that as attained in its sojourn in the environment.

Venus makes for that which becomes the bright or shining light in the experience, and in its development; that is, its love for its fellow man, and the manner, the way, that it would make for the greater education—or application of education—in the experiences of individuals; as well as love for children, love for those that have their problems and their stumbling in their own selves and in those things that make for the experiences of problems in their own activities.

As to what the entity has accomplished, or may accomplish in the experience in the present as respecting these urges, has depended and will depend upon what is the basis of its ideal. Not as an idealist, but rather as one making the application of the motivative forces towards constructive influences in the experience of individuals as associated with the activity of the entity in its relationships with others.

Editor's Note: The following readings are all for the same person, case #900.

Reading 900-6

Yes, we have the records here as have to do with the life and destiny of the entity, irrespective of the will's forces in the life. This is as being influenced irrespective of the will, that factor determining the life, the destiny of each entity. In this we find one coming under the influence of those conditions as are given in the effect of that planet, upon which the entity had its sojourn, being one in Mercury—with the influences to the good of Jupiter—Neptune—with the adverse influence of Saturn, and Uranus, when at the square of Saturn and Mars. This we find in opposition to much that would be given in knowledge, as given, from the aspects of the influences as given today. See?

In this we find the influences—one given to being a leader in every condition regarding those of the mental understanding of conditions. One being given to be directed—yet never driven to any condition. May be led, especially through respect and many conditions in others, or through the ennobling influence of either love or respect, yet never driven in either. One given to have much of the worldly goods, for [he is] under the influence of Neptune's forces and under the direction of Jupiter's forces, which make the ennobling influence in the Earth's plane.

The entity in its thirty-fifth year will find much of the worldly goods in its possession, unless willed outwardly from such conditions, see?

It will be the natural influence coming from conditions that have to do with those of the watery nature, or from the sea. One that should be ever in its labors near large bodies of water, for Neptune's forces, as there exercised, are mental and not mystic forces comes through development from the water nature, see? Through the moon's elements [we find these] bring the forces in love affairs to deter these conditions, one that is given to thinking lightly of the heart's forces—and should only be in domestic relations late in life, see?

As conditions in the financial have been set forth, body is one that will give much of the influence in the mental forces to others. One upon whom many will rely for their mental activities in the Earth's forces.

One that is given especially to being the control in many financial undertakings . . .

In the next return we would find the body through its will and spirit force need not be in Earth's plane again.

Reading 900-14

Yes, we have these conditions as were made, and the co-relation of these with past, present and future conditions regarding this entity, [900].

We find there are many of the conditions, as were outlined in this, have had the influence that to the receptive mental faculties of the entity are apparent in the present existence, and many more will follow . . .

(Q) *As given in the horoscope, the body [900] is influenced adversely, or to the bad, when the planets Saturn and Uranus are at the square of Saturn and Mars. Give us, please, the dates when this will occur.*

(A) Last occurrence, and the effects apparent in this entity's condition, 19th day of August, 1924. Will occur again on the 13th day of June, 1925. Again in January 2, 1926. Again in October 4, 1926.

These passages are also influenced by other astronomical conditions. Hence vary in their intensity. This, as we find, varies then the condition of the influence, or of that portion of the entity, as it were, so tempered and tempted.

(Q) *Of what particular bad influence should this body be warned of when next the square of these planets occur?*

(A) That of the influence of wrath towards some individual whom will be in close relation with the entity's business connection, that has to do with aerial corporations. Do not allow the temper to find the manifestation in physical action. Through will control wrath.

(Q) *How may he lessen the bad influence to himself?*

(A) Use of will.

(Q) *How may he use his will to allow the good influence of Jupiter and Neptune to fully operate to work to the body's greater good, financially, physically and spiritually?*

(A) In Jupiter's forces we find those great ennobling, those conditions that would bring the monies and forces of good in the life.

In Neptune, those of the mysticism, mystery, spiritual insight, spiritual development.

The Mercury influence of mental understanding of each.

Then, with the mental insight into the operative elements of ennobling, of virtues, of good, of beautiful, with the mysteries of the universal forces, given understanding, brings the development to soul's forces. For the soul feeds upon that environment to which the mental guides and directs, and the expectancy is that soul development that each entity must exercise through will.

(Q) *Are there particular times when Moon's influences are particularly strong, and thereby counteract the good influences of Jupiter and Neptune, to bring worldly goods to body's possession? How may he use will to avoid these adverse influences?*

(A) In Moon's influence in this entity has particularly to do with the earthly satisfaction of desire toward opposite sex, in the present plane's sphere. These we find are at times adverse to ennobling forces, and may be made to appear in self to coincide with mysteries of life; using will then to know that each and every such condition must be brought under those forces of Jupiter and Neptune, that this influence, through will, will be turned into that which will bring the better conditions in the life's plane. For with the mental carrying such conditions of any intrigue against ennobling influence in earth's plane, or carrying such intrigue that bring the mysteries of life to naught, these we see work condemnation rather than blessings in the life of an entity. Hence the warnings as given of the Moon's influence at times in the [entity's condition in the] earth's plane. Will used directly. Warding against such conditions becoming detrimental to the body's development.

(Q) Did this entity have its sojourn in Mercury prior to the present appearance on Earth?

(A) It did.

(Q) Is the body now living and developing in the will and spirit forces such as the body need not return to earth plane?

(A) It is.

(Q) How may the body improve so as to better get good results from the good influence of Mercury, Jupiter and Neptune?

(A) As has been given. All spoken from the astronomical point or vision. In mental declare the ennobling, the good, the mysteries of mental, of life, and thus give the better influence, insight, the better conditions from which [there may be] the expectancy of the soul for its development. See? Simple, easy of understanding, when once gained the insight to same.

Reading 900-179

Mrs. Cayce: You will have before you information as given regarding [900] in a reading on the 27th day of December, 1924, especially that concerning the adverse influence in his life that would occur about January 2,1926. You will please tell us what will be the nature of this adversity, or *how* he may *prevent* such conditions, and *when* will this occur again, according to the information as has been given. You will please answer this in full detail.

Mr. Cayce: Yes. This we have is as seen from that influence of the squares of adverse planetary influences, or that astrological aspect as is presented in the life of entity, which has its bearing as pertaining to the will's application in the present sphere, see? This, as we see, will present through that again of madness (temper, see?). Rather as that of a disappointing condition presenting itself in the condition, life or action of individuals, see? The aspect of same in will's forces is protected . . . by spiritual developments in the entity, and then this would be the source through which the overcoming of same may be helped, see? That is, the application to self of those influences of will, with the law as pertains to that of right for right's sake and its influence in the life of the individual as pertains to self or *any* through whom there may a disappointment be presented to same.

5

●

Planetary Sojourns

Editor's Note: One of the most fascinating concepts to come through Edgar Cayce's discourses were his teachings about soul activity between Earth incarnations and how these affect our present lives. Here are some of these discourses.

Reading 1895-1

. . . the experiences of the entity in the interims of planetary sojourns between the earthly manifestations become the innate mental urges, that may or may not at times be a part of the day dreaming, or the thought and meditation of the inmost self.

Hence we find astrological aspects and influence in the experience, but rather because of the entity's sojourn in the environ than because of a certain star, constellation or even zodiacal sign being in such and such a position at the time of birth.

Know that man—as has been expressed—was given dominion over all, and in the understanding of same may use all of the laws as pertaining to same for his benefit.

In the application of same as a benefit—if it is for self-indulgence or self-expression alone, it loses its own individuality in the personality of that sought or desired; and thus the very knowledge may be used as a stumbling-stone. But if each experience is as a manifestation to the glory of a creative or heavenly force, or that which is continual thus the judgements being drawn from an ideal that is spiritual in its concept, then there is the greater growth, the greater harmony—for there becomes an at-onement with the influences about same.

Reading 281-55

(Q) *Through other planetary sojourns an entity has the opportunity to change its rate of vibration so as to be attracted in the earth plane under another soul number.*

(A) Each planetary influence vibrates at a different rate of vibration. An entity entering that influence enters that vibration; not necessary that he change, but it is the grace of God that he may! It is part of the universal consciousness, the universal law.

Reading 1947-1

In giving the urges, then, we find that the astrological influences are not so much because of the certain position of the Sun or the Moon or the Stars, but because of their relationship which is a relativity of influence or force; for, being from the body or materialization, there is the activity of the soul in the environs in which certain influences have been and are accredited to the activities from those planetary sojourns. Thus they become as signs, omens in the experience.

Reading 2599-1

In giving the interpretations of the records as we find them here, these are chosen with the desire and purpose that this be a helpful experience for the entity; enabling it to better fulfill that purpose for which it entered this experience.

Know that one's manifestations in the earth are not by chance but a fulfillment of those purposes the Creative Forces have with each individual entity.

For, the Creative Influence is mindful ever, and hath not willed that any soul should perish, but hath with every temptation prepared a way, a means of escape.

Thus the very fact of a material manifestation should become an awareness to the individual entity of the mindfulness of that influence of Creative Energy in the experience.

Then, as to the abilities with this entity—magnify the virtues, minimize the faults—not only in your judgments of others. For with what judgment ye mete, it will be meted to thee again.

Thus the purpose of each experience is that the entity may magnify and glorify that which is good. For, good is of the one source, God, and is eternal.

Then as an individual entity magnifies that which is good, and minimizes that which is false, it grows in grace, in knowledge, in understanding.

Know that in the manner ye mete, or do to thy fellow man, so ye do unto thy Maker.

Then let it be from this premise that the judgments and the activities of this entity in this material experience may be drawn as a helpful force in its journey through this particular sojourn.

From the sources of the previous sojourns we find urges arising materially in the experience of the entity—that is, from the previous earthly sojourns as well as the astrological sojourns during the interims between earthly manifestations.

Not that there are influences from the position of stars, planets or the like that may not be met; but these are as urges—just as the environs of an individual in the material plane produce urges, because of studies or activities in a given direction, and because certain material abilities are innately a part of the entity's experience. Yet urges oft arise in the experience of an entity for this or that, the source of which the entity itself may not understand or comprehend—for no one in the family thought or acted in that direction.

Then, this—the environ of the entity, the soul manifesting in the earth—may be called by another name, as with this entity—a part of the present name in the experience before this; and the abilities as an individual to meet others, to influence them in the activities in which certain interests might be magnified, come from the entity's activities in the previous sojourn.

Thus the earthly sojourns make for manifested urges in the present experience. Also those planetary sojourns, in this present solar system, make for urges that are accredited to those particular planets as states of consciousness—that become innately manifested in the present entity.

For instance, in this entity we find the manifestation of Mercury, Venus, Jupiter, Uranus—manifested and latent in the dreams, the visions, the activities; in the high mental abilities of the entity, the ability to reason things through, the stableness of its activity in using not only material but mental forces as an influence to urge others to buy or to be interested in, or to analyze conditions.

Thus in the present, and manifestedly so, the entity might find the abilities as an adjuster, or as an individual to give expression as to evaluation of materials or properties, or abilities of individuals.

In Venus we find that appreciation of the beautiful, as related to art, as related to things, as related to conditions in the relationships of groups of peoples one to another.

Also from Jupiter we find the association with groups, masses, as a reflection in the activities of abilities, and that in which the entity may apply itself in the present experience.

Uranus brings the extremes, in which the entity may rise to great heights of expectation and yet at times find self in a wonderment. Yet innately there are those expectancies in spiritual facts, in the occult, in the psychic forces, that are powers of might for either good or evil. For, as indicated, in Uranus there are the extremes.

Know, as from the first premise, that no influence surpasses the WILL of an individual. The power of will is that birthright as the gift from the Creative Force to each entity, that it may become one with that Influence; knowing itself to be itself yet a part of and one with the Creative Influence as the directing influence in the experience.

Also the earthly sojourns bring urges through the latent faculties of the sensory forces; or they become characteristics that may be indicated—either latent or manifested—as the power or might manifesting; for only as the entity works with or against an influence does it become magnified in the experiences of the entity.

Reading 243-10

In entering, we find, astrologically, the entity coming under the influence of Mercury, Mars, Jupiter, Venus, and Neptune. These, as we find, have builded, and have influenced the entity, in the present experience. Also we find urges as respecting the experiences as related to innate urges, and that as has been *builded* in the present entity.

[Aside:] Let not this be confusing, as to innate urges and that as is builded in the present experience, for the application of will, and of innate urge through planetary influences, is exercised in this entity as we would find it in few.

In the experience, then, we find these as builded *irrespective* of will, and those that have been builded as respecting the *application* of will's influence; for *will* is that developing factor with which an entity chooses or builds that freedom, or that of being free, knowing the truth as is applicable in the experience, and in the various experiences as has been builded; for that builded must be met, whether in thought or in deed; for thoughts are deeds, and their current run is through the whole of the influence in an *entity's* experience. Hence, as was given, "He that hateth his brother has committed as great a sin as he that slayeth a man," for the deed is as of an accomplishment in the mental being, which is the builder for every entity.

Much has been met, much as been *builded* by the entity in the present experience. Much has been experienced by the entity in the various spheres through which the entity has passed.

In that builded, we find one of high, ennobling ideas and ideals; often tempered in Mars, through wrath, that has brought does bring, will bring, many of the experiences that have been experienced in the building of the entity's inner being to the action within the life.

In those influences in Jupiter, finds for the bigness of the entity's vision, the broadness of the good or bad that may be wielded in the influence of those whom the entity contacts from time to time, or period to period, or experience to experience.

In those influences seen in those of Neptune, brings for those of that as is of the *mystery* in the experiences of the entity; the associations in many peculiar circumstances and conditions; the conditions and experiences, and influences, as bring many conditions as, by others, would be misunderstood (and there *be* minds that would misunderstand, rather than know the truth).

In the experiences there has been *innately* built, the fear of evil in the life, the fear of those that would bring condemnation on those who are in power, and oft is the entity too *good* to others for its own good!

Through the attempt innate to build that which would be the releasing of those experiences which have been had by the entity.

In those influences seen in Neptune, also brings that water—large *bodies* of water—the entity will gain most through the experience, has gained and will gain, through sojourn near, or passing over, large bodies of water, and *salt* water is preferable; for in the experiences will be seen, fresh hasn't *always* meant for living water.

In those as builded innately, we find:

One that is in that position of making friends easily, and just as easily losing same; yet there are friendships made that make for the better understanding in the experience, and in those of *Venus* forces comes the love that is *innate* in the experience of the entity. Through all the vicissitudes of life this remaineth, for the entity has gained much that makes for that as was given—"There is a friend that sticketh closer than a brother," and "he that is just kind to the least of these, my little ones, is greater than he that hath taken a mighty city." These building, these kept within the consciousness of the entity, will build to that Christ consciousness as makes all free; for in Him is the life, and He is the light that shineth into the dark places, even to the recesses of that of His own consciousness that makes for that which casteth out fear; (for being afraid is the first consciousness of sin's entering in, for he that is made afraid has lost consciousness of self's own heritage with the Son; for we are heirs through Him to that Kingdom that is beyond all that that would make afraid, or that would cause a doubt in the heart of any. Through the recesses of the heart, then, search out that that would make afraid, casting out fear, and *He* alone may guide.)

Reading 137–4

In this we find, with the influences of the solar systems, there are many elements that enter to make this rather an exceptional entity in the present earth plane, for at the time of the birth, (though the soul took its flight from Mercury, and this brings especially vivid understandings in a material world of definite conditions) there were so many influences in the house of birth that the body partakes of those influences that were experienced in other spheres and planes, and brings them to the present earth's forces and may, with the knowledge and understanding, be able to manifest many of the unseen forces in the earth's plane. These special influences being Mercury, Uranus, Jupiter, Venus. These all bring extraordinary vivid conditions, yet with the mental forces, especially in the conditions of Mercury, this gives exceptional forces to the entity in many respects. Also we find the Sun and Arcturus, the greater Sun, giving of the strength in mental and spiritual elements toward developing of soul and of the attributes toward the better forces in earth's spheres. This brings, especially, the conditions of these characters:

One that is exceptional in many ways, manners and faculties, especially in those of mental forces having great vision in every direction, especially those of the unseen elements, bringing then much psychic and occult forces to the body.

The highest conception of all domestic relations, the highest conceptions of honor. The highest conceptions of respect. The highest conceptions in every relation in friendship and in every element relating to others.

Editor's Note: The group working with Edgar Cayce attempted to develop tests that would help individuals identify their planetary influences and their past-life influences. Cayce said that only the astrological was attainable, given that past lives required reading the Akashic Record of a soul or the soul awakening to its memories of past lives. He guided them to use this astrological information for helping to identify one's vocation. Here is that reading.

TEXT OF READING 5753-3

This Psychic Reading given by Edgar Cayce at his home on Arctic Crescent, Virginia Beach, Va., this 25th day of October, 1939, in accordance with request made by Hugh Lynn Cayce, Manager of the Ass'n for Research & Enlightenment, Inc.

PRESENT

Edgar Cayce; Gertrude Cayce, Conductor; Gladys Davis, Steno. Hugh Lynn Cayce.

READING

Time of Reading 11:30 to 11:40 A. M. Eastern Standard Time.

Mrs. Cayce: You will have before you the psychic work of Edgar Cayce relative to information from Life Readings concerning vocational guidance; together with the entity, the enquiring mind, Hugh Lynn Cayce, present here, who seeks to correlate and use such information. From a study of the Life Readings it would seem that an individual's mental and spiritual development, his contentment, is dependent upon releasing and expression of basic mental and emotional urges coming from planetary sojourns and past incarnations. Please give at this time suggestions for the development of a system or a series of intelligence tests which will reveal these basic urges and help an individual in selecting a life's work. It is hoped that such information as may be given here may be developed and used through scout activities and the Princess Anne Schools. You will answer questions.

Mr. Cayce: Yes, we have the information here, that has been indicated in Life Readings as to vocational guidance for individuals.

In developing a plan, or a manner of seeking ways in which individuals might give expression of the latent faculties and powers from the material sojourns, as well as the planetary influences—here we will find that there are conflicting forces and influences at times—as we have indicated.

The astrological aspects may give a tendency, an inclination; and a systematic, scientific study of same would indicate the vocation. And about eighty percent of the individuals would be in the position of being influenced by such astrological aspects; or would be in the position for their abilities to be indicated from same.

But the other twenty percent would not be in that position, due to the influences from activity or the use of their abilities in material experience. Hence in these it would be not only necessary that their material sojourns be given, but as to what had been accomplished through same, and that to be met in the present experience. For, as has been indicated, no influence—astrologically or from material sojourns—surpasses the will or the determination of the individual. Then, there are material factors that rule or govern or direct or influence such forces. These may be tempered by the astrological aspects, but these are not (the astrological aspects) the major influence or force—the will.

Thus, only about eighty percent of the individuals may have their abilities indicated from the astrological aspects in the direction of vocational guidance, as to be a determining factor for such.

If some five individuals would be taken, and their charts or astrological aspects indicated, and questions asked as to determining the influence or force from same—from such an aspect there might be given information so that a general chart might be indicated for a questionnaire, or a test, or an activity that would be of material benefit in a great *number* of individuals—but never a perfect score may be indicated. For the will, as well as the factors of environment, have their influence.

Ready for questions.

(Q) How can the urges from past incarnations be determined by a test or series of tests?

(A) As just indicated—this may only be done by giving the material sojourns of the individual. But if the astrological aspects and influences are given, then there may be determined a questionnaire from same.

(Q) Should the chart be drawn from the geocentric or the heliocentric system?

(A) The geocentric system would be the more in keeping with the Persian force or influence.

(Q) Any other suggestion to Hugh Lynn Cayce regarding the development of this at this time?

(A) As indicated, there may be charts drawn of five individuals, and a questionnaire may be determined for factors in the individual experience—as to what their inclinations or activities are. Not by telling, but by questioning!

Then *from* same, as indicated, there may be given a more correct or direct questionnaire that would be helpful for a large *number* of individuals—but *not* a perfect score.

For in about twenty percent of the populace at the present time, it is dependent upon what the individuals have done with their urges *through* material sojourns.

As indicated through this channel, some are in keeping with the astrological charts, others are found to be partially so, others are diametrically opposed to same—because of the activities of the individuals.

We are through for the present.

Editor's Note: Mr. Cayce's discourses state that all souls were created at the same moment, yet he used the term *old soul* occasionally. He

later explained that he meant a soul that had been sojourning in and around the Earth for many lifetimes. The following is a reading for an old soul, and this reading has many interesting references to planetary and constellational sojourning.

TEXT OF READING 436-2 M 28 (Elevator Boy, Christian with East Indian leaning)

This psychic reading given by Edgar Cayce at Lillian Edgerton, Inc., 267 Fifth Ave., N.Y.C., this 10th day of November, 1933, in accordance with request made by self—Mr. [436], Active Member of the Ass'n for Research & Enlightenment, Inc.

P R E S E N T

Edgar Cayce; Hugh Lynn Cayce, Conductor; Gladys Davis, Steno. Mr. [436].

R E A D I N G

Born March 29, 1905, (11:30 p.m.) in Midland, Virginia.

Time of Reading 3:00 to 3:50 p.m. Eastern Standard Time. . . . , D.C.

(Life Reading Suggestion)

Mr. Cayce: Yes, we have the entity and those relations with the universe and universal forces, that are latent and exhibited in the personalities of the present entity, [436].

It would be well to comment upon the oldness of this soul, especially in its activities—as will be seen—in periods when the occult and mystic influences were manifested in the experience of the entity in the earth; and make for influences that have been (or may be made) very good or very bad in the experience of the entity. Hence, this is an old soul.

In giving the personalities and the individuality of the entity in the present experience, we must approach same from the astrological, though these in the very fact of that given respecting its activities in the earth during such periods when such changes or activities were manifested in the material affairs of individuals, make for little that may be compulsory in astrological influence. Yet *impulses* arise from these influences.

As in passing from Pisces into Aries, there are those influences innately and manifested in the mental forces of the body; much of both of these, and they become conflicting in the experience at times of the entity.

Pisces brings rather the mystery and creative forces, and magnanimous aspects in students of—or in the thought of—influences in the active principles of individual impulse; with Aries bringing reason, or air, or airy actions, yet reason, more than Pisces would make the demands in the self at time for reasons for every manifestation, whether material conditions, mental or spiritual conditions in the experience of the entity. And at other periods it may be said that the entity becomes rather susceptible to influences about the body, without considering seriously the sources of the information and as to whether same is able to be verified by others or not. Feelings of same impress the entity from this astrological influence, which—as we see—does not only control earth's sojourn but the position of the entity in this sojourn through the planetary influences in the earth's solar system.

As to the sojourns in the astrological influences then, we find these are the ruling; not from their position at the birth, but rather from the position of the entity's activities in that environ.

Mars is an influence rather from the associations then, in self's own experience. Or when dissensions, distrust, dissatisfaction, madness, wars, arise; these come *about* the entity rather than influencing the *activities* of the entity, other than through the associations with individuals that make demands upon the entity and its activities in these directions. These become at times concrete experiences in the entity's activities in the present experience; yet these, as we find, for many a year now (and these began some three years ago) will be less in the experience until Mars in '38 or '39 becomes nearer in its influence upon the sojourners of those in the earth that have experienced a sojourn in that environ.

Hence this may be said, in a manner, to be of little influence then in the period, or during that period, when the entity should make for a stabilization in self's experience of that to which it may develop its better abilities in this present sojourn in the earth.

From Venus rather a complex position or condition comes to the experience of the entity, where filial or marital or such relations as of loves in the material earth come in the experience. Not that there hasn't been, nor won't be, nor isn't existent, that which is pure, elevating and helpful in the experience of the entity in its relationships with individuals of both sexes in this way and manner; yet these have brought some very pleasant experiences and some very contrary and contradictory influences in the activities and in the experience of the entity in the present.

Hence it may be given in passing, to the entity, that the love of and for a pure body is the most sacred experience in an entity's earth sojourn; yet these conditions soured, these conditions turned into vitrol, may become the torments of an exemplary body, and one well-meaning, and make for loss of purposes.

Keep the friendships, then. Keep those relationships that are founded upon all that is constructive in earth, in the mind, in the spirit.

As to those influences from the sojourn of the entity in Uranian forces, as may be indicated from that given as to the oldness and as to the delving into the occult and mystic and the application in the experience, the entity has sojourned more than once in this environ and under quite varied or different experiences and manifestations. Hence there are periods when earthly conditions, mental conditions, spiritual conditions, are very good; and others when all are very bad in the experience of the entity in the present. Yet, as we find, in the application of self as related to the impulses that may rise in the consciousness of the entity in the present experience from those impulses received from the sojourns, these may be made the strong fort in the activities of self in the present. But they must be tempered, from the very experiences in the sojourn, to making for not an active force in those experiences from planetary influences in a weak body, but turn to strengthening the body-physical for the manifestations of the correct raising of those vital energies in the material body, through which such influences may make for manifestations and experiences in the earth's sojourn. These influences from Uranus make for many of the ills that have been in the experience in the body, in the nervous reactions to the physical body, to the weak experiences to the physical body, when the very vital life force of a material body was in danger of being separated from physical for an ethereal sojourn.

As to the appearances, then, and their influence in the present, these are given as the ones influencing the activities of the present body; rather than numbers, we give those that make for the greater activity in the present:

Before this we find the entity was in the land of nativity, and about those places, those peoples, where the first settlings were—and the first sojournings that spread beyond the mere force builded; or about that town that was the first capitol of this new land, or this portion of same. And among the activities there are many of those things being reconstructed, re-enacted, that will be not only of physical interest but will, with the application of the abilities within self, recall to the entity many of the associations that the entity had with the peoples of the land (native). While the entity did not go what is proverbially called "native" in the experience, the associations were such, with those that acted in the capacity of the spiritual leaders (or with what were termed the medicine men of the period), and with those that later attempted to set themselves as leaders of this people, that the entity made friends both with the natives and the colonists, aiding the colonists in the period to establish better relations; in the name then Edward Compton, a distant family name even that may be found among those that sojourned in the peninsula land of that portion of the country.

The entity lost and gained through the experience; gained in the application of self for the benefiting of those with whom the entity sojourned, and the natives also whom the entity aided in making better cooperative relationships in the activities of the people of the period and time. The entity aided in establishing such relationships that there was the trading of the native peoples in distant lands. One particular period of interest, that may be noted in history, was when the entity aided in bringing to the peoples corn from the western portion of their native land, that sustained those peoples through a very bad period.

From that period there is the influence oft in the present in those activities when studies of those peoples are the experience of the entity, and there are both confusing and constructive influences. Yet, when about many of a mediumistic turn, many of those with whom the entity engaged in life and activity would attempt to speak to the entity; especially one that termed himself Big Rock, Black Rock.

Before this we find the entity was during that period when there were the returnings of those peoples in the land now called Greece, from the rebellions that had been active in Mesopotamia and in the regions about what is known as Turkey and those lands; during those periods of Xenophon's activities and those wars.

The entity was among the few of these natives, strong in body, purposeful in intent, to return to the native land; and the entity gained through the experience but lost in the latter portion of the sojourn when returning to the native land, when power was entrusted in the activities of the entity; and while the purposefulness was correct, there arose those that distrusted and brought contentions by the accusations brought against the entity, in the name Xerxion. Then Xerxion lost in faith in his fellow man, and the faith in the purposefulness of those that were attributing to the gods, or the powers and forces as they were named and termed, the elements to maintain the equilibrium. Hence in that the entity lost, and in the present—while there are those abilities in self to lead for a purposefulness in its activity, too oft has the entity become discouraged when accusations of unkind things were brought, or when experiences made for the losing of confidences in friends and associates it has made discouragements too easily in the experience in the present. This (in passing, may be said) is a test period for the entity in its relationship, particularly. Hence the entity should turn to the abilities within and find self first, knowing in what, in whom the entity has believed; knowing He is able to keep that which is committed unto Him against any experience that may arise in the lives or activities of those who are His loved ones, His chosen. Who has He chosen? They that do His biddings. What are His biddings? Love the Lord thy God with all thine heart (and thy God meaning Him that in Spirit is the Creative Forces of all that is manifested), keeping self unspotted from the world or any smirch of activity, and loving thy neighbor, thy brother, as thine self. These will make for the relieving of all those influences in the experience, and bring harmony, peace, joy, understanding, in the experience of the entity; and will enable the entity to not only study, not only to understand, but—best of all—to comprehend from what source many of those influences arise, as we will see has to do upon the mental body of the entity, and become active oft in the physical forces or the physical activities through their nerve reflexes in a material body.

Before this we find the entity was in that land now known as the Egyptian, during that period when there was the returning of those that had been astrayed through the sending away of the priest of the land.

The entity was among those that were banished with the priest, being with the priest Ra-Ta in the association and in the activities of gathering together the tenets that the scribe—in a way; rather the one gathering the data than one scribing or protecting the data—collected. The entity aided the priest specifically in some of the associations and connections with those of the temple gatherers to whom the priest gave heart and mind; and for the act among those the entity was severely punished when banished by the natives, rather than the king. Yet, being healed by the priest in the foreign land, the entity came again into Egypt when there was the re-establishing, and aided in rebuilding the temples of service; being active then in what today would be called the preparations for those things that kept the cleansings of the temple after use of individual in body, or as a caretaker (termed in the present) of offices, temples, churches or buildings. Then the entity was in the name Pth-Lerr. The entity gained and gained, and much that is suffered in body is as a bringing to bear of that which may make the mental contact with the tenets of the experience.

One might ask (this aside, please), why would such be brought to bear? Because, with the experience of the entity in the period, seeing the developments and the activities, there was set within the soul that desire: "Come what may, whatever is necessary in my whole experience of my soul, make me to know again the joys of the tenets of Ra-Ta."

In the present these may mean much, if they are builded for a soul development in the present; for these needs be to overcome those experiences in the sojourn just previous in the Atlantean land.

Before this we find the entity in the Atlantean land rather rebelled with those forces of Baalilal, with those activities in the electrical appliances, when these were used by those peoples to make for beautiful buildings without but temples of sin within.

The entity, in the name Saail, was a priest (demoted) in the Temple of Oz in Atlantis, and lost from soul development, gained from material things; yet these fade, these make raids upon the body in physical manifestations. These make for hindrances in activity in that known within the innate self. For, rather were the mysteries of the black arts as applied in the experience practiced by Saail, yet these in the present may be turned into account in material things in making material connections; but use or apply same in the experience rather in the mental and spiritual manner for the soul development of the entity, rather than for materiality in the present. These are weaknesses, then, yet weakness is only strength misapplied or used in vain ways.

Before this we find the entity was in that land that has been termed Zu, or Lemuria, or Mu. This was before the sojourn of peoples in perfect body form; rather when they may be said to have been able to—through those developments of the period—be in the body or out of the body and act upon materiality. In the spirit or in flesh these made those things, those influences, that brought destruction; for the atmospheric pressure in the earth in the period was quite different from that experienced by the physical being of today.

The entity then was in the name Mmuum, or rather those calls that make easy the mysteries of words as related to sounds and rote that bring to the consciousness, in those that have indwelled in those lands, that activity that merits (not the word), that brings, that impulse that urges that those forces from without act upon the elements in whatever sphere they may bring a material manifestation. This must be controlled within self, from those influences in [436]; for these are those things at times that hinder.

Let self, then, be grounded rather in the faith of that which is, was, and ever will be, the source of all spirit, all thought all mind, all physical manifestation—the *one* God, as called in this period. In that period he was called Zu-u-u-u-u; in the next Ohm—Oh-u-m; in the next (now known as Egypt) with Ra-Ta, He was called God—G-o-r-r-d!

As to the abilities of the entity, and that to which it may attain, and how, in the present:

First it may be said, study—through that known in self of the spiritual and mental forces active in the experience of the body—to show self approved unto an ideal that is set in the Son, the Christ, knowing that in possessing the consciousness of His love, His manifestation, all is well; for, as is known, without that love as He manifested among men, nothing can, nothing did, nothing will come into consciousness of matter. Not that we may deny evil and banish it, but supplanting and rooting out evil in the experience, replacing same with the love that is in the consciousness of the body Jesus, the Christ, we may do all things in His name; and using those opportunities in whatsoever sphere of activity the entity may find to show forth those commands He gave, "If ye love me, keep my commandments." What, ye ask, are His commandments? "A new commandment give I unto you, that ye love one another." What, then, are the fruits of love? The fruits of the spirit; which are kindness, hope, fellowship, brotherly love, friendship, patience; these are the fruits of the spirit; these are the commands of Him that ye manifest them in whatsoever place ye find yourself, and your soul shall grow in grace, in knowledge, in understanding, and that joy that comes with a perfect knowledge in Him brings the joys of earth, the joys of the mental mind, or joys of the spheres, and the *glory* of the Father in thine experience.

Ready for questions.

(Q) *When will adverse planetary change for better influences in my life?*

(A) As indicated, the receding of Mars brings, and has brought, better planetary influences; as the mental activities and applications in the light of the love in Christ brings with those activities in the coming closer and closer of Venus with Uranus; which begins in December, present year, for the approach, reaching nearer conjunction in May or June of the coming year better conditions, mentally, materially, financially.

(Q) *What is the main purpose of this incarnation?*

(A) To set self aright as respecting the variations in those tenets in the first two experiences in the sojourn, tempered in those tenets given in Ra-Ta—that, "The Lord Thy God is *One!*" And manifesting of that oneness in the little things makes the soul grow in His grace!

We are through for the present.

Editor's Note: Mr. Cayce even gave readings on how to subdue negative influences from planetary or astrological soul activity. Here is one example.

TEXT OF READING 137-18 M 27
(Stockbroker, Hebrew)

This psychic reading given by Edgar Cayce at his office, 322 Grafton Avenue, Dayton, Ohio, this 24th day of July, 1925, in accordance with request made by self—Mr. [137].

P R E S E N T

Edgar Cayce; Mrs. Cayce, Conductor; Gladys Davis, Steno.

R E A D I N G

Born October 28, 1898, in New York City. On the floor of Time of Reading the New York Stock 9:30 a.m. Dayton Savings Time. Exchange, Wall & New Streets, N.Y.

Mrs. Cayce: You will have before you the body of [137], on the floor of the N.Y. Stock Exchange, Wall & New Streets, New York City, N.Y., with the information as has been given this body in readings given for same on the 28th day of October, 1924, also that given on the 12th day of January, 1925, [see 137–4 & 137–12] especially that portion of same relating to the undue influences in the life of [137] when Moon's forces square to Saturn and Mars bring doubts within the body's mental forces. This is given in reading of January 12th, as occurring in the week of August 13, 1925. You will please tell us just the character of influence that will occur, whether of mental, spiritual or physical forces, and how this entity may guard against this influence.

Mr. Cayce: Yes, we have the body here, and the information as has been given this body in regards to influences as are exercised in the life of the entity at the periods given, through position of the planetary forces as are exercised in the life of same.

Now, we find that with the indwelling urges as are seen within the individual, when there occur certain positions of those planetary influences under which the body (meaning spiritual force body) has developed, these bring the intense urge towards those experiences of the entity as it passed through that phase of its development, for we find the urge within each entity is its experiences in all phases of its existence, plus the environmental conditions of body at time, with the will of entity counterbalancing same through body–mind urge. Hence the necessity of each entity understanding, having knowledge of those laws that do govern same in the material or physical realm, as well as those pertaining to the spiritual forces as are manifest through the body in each of its various changes, for we find all are one, for the real body is that spiritual force manifesting in same, always through the Trinity of that comprising same.

In the information as has been given as we find, these influences come for this body at this particular or special time, when through the influences as are exercised in the position Moon, Jupiter, with Saturn and with Mars, this brings to that body, [137], those of that urge, that doubt of self and self's abilities to manifest either mental (Moon with Saturn), with physical, (doubting of own physical health, see?) through the forces or powers in Mars, the own spiritual forces as is the influence, or undue influence on Jupiter's forces with this position as manifested. Then, we find these at this time pertaining to this nature:

The body-mind, the spiritual-mind, has reached at this period, especially, and during week of August 13, 1925, that place where the doubts of every nature, pertaining to this threefold force as is given here, come to the body. Hence, we will find, will be easily aggravated through any mental association, whether in business relation, moral relations socially or marital relations, for, seemingly, at this time would occur all of these combining with one to bring the detrimental forces to the mind. With the condition of mind comes that condition where the physical forces, apparently, respond more to these of the conditions wherein weaknesses are shown or manifested in same. Then the combination of all would bring as to that—well—"I don't care! What difference does it make? Let it go to pot!"—See?

Then, to overcome this, rather place those forces as are manifest through will forces, knowing that these do appear. That, "Get thee behind me Saturn (Satan), that I *will* serve the living God, with *my* body, *my* mind, *my* money, *my* spirit, *my* soul, for I am *His*, and through *me*, my body, my mind, do I manifest *my* impression, *my* interpretation of *my* God."

This does, not, as we see, relate to physical accidents, physical conditions, physical things, pertaining to the material things of life, save as would be affected by same through—"Well, I don't care."

We are through for the present.

Editor's Note: This next reading used Edgar Cayce's soul as an example, explaining his soul journey, which includes physical incarnations and planetary sojourns.

Reading 5755-1

Mrs. Cayce: In all Life Readings given through this channel there are references to sojourns of the soul-entity between incarnations on the earth plane, in various planes of consciousness represented by the other planets in our solar system. You will give at this time a discourse which will explain what takes place in soul development in each of these states of consciousness in their order relative to the evolution of the soul; explaining what laws govern this movement from plane to plane, their influence on life in this earth plane and what if any relationship these planes have to astrology. Questions.

Mr. Cayce: Yes, we have the information and sources from which same may be obtained as to individual experiences, sojourns and their influence.

As we find, in attempting to give a coherent explanation of that as may be sought, or as may be made applicable in the experience of individuals who seek to apply such information, it is well that an individual soul-entity, the record of whose astrological and earthly sojourns you have, be used as an example.

Then a comparison may be drawn for those who would judge same from the astrological aspects, as well as from the astrological or planetary sojourns of such individuals.

What better example may be used, then, than this entity with whom you are dealing [Edgar Cayce, File #294].

Rather than the aspects of the material sojourn, then, we would give them from the astrological:

From an astrological aspect, then, the greater influence at the entrance of this entity that ye call Cayce was from Uranus. Here we find the extremes. The sojourn in Uranus was arrived at from what type of experience or activity of the entity? As Bainbridge [in a previous incarnation], the entity in the material sojourn was a wastrel, one who considered only self; having to know the extremes in the own experience as well as others. Hence the entity was drawn to that environ. Or, how did the Master put it? "As the tree falls, so does it lie." [Eccl. 11:3 by Solomon. John's Note? Where did Jesus say it?] Then in the Uranian sojourn there are the influences from the astrological aspects of *extremes*; and counted in thy own days from the very position of that attunement, that tone, that color. For it is not strange that music, color, vibration are all a part of the planets, just as the planets are a part—and a pattern—of the whole universe. Hence to that attunement which it had merited, which it had meted in itself, was the entity drawn for the experience. What form, what shape?

The birth of the entity into Uranus was not from the earth into Uranus, but from those stages of consciousness through which each entity or soul passes. It passes into oblivion as it were, save for its consciousness that there is a way, there is a light, there is an understanding, there have been failures and there are needs for help. Then help *consciously* is sought!

Hence the entity passes along those stages that some have seen as planes, some have seen as steps, some have seen as cycles, and some have experienced as places.

How far? How far is tomorrow to any soul? How far is yesterday from thy consciousness?

You are *in* same (that is, all time as one time), yet become gradually aware of it; passing through, then, as it were, God's record or book of consciousness or of remembrance; for meeting, being measured out as it were to that to which thou hast attained.

Who hath sought? Who hath understood?

Only they that seek shall find!

Then, born in what body? That as befits that plane of consciousness; the *extremes*, as ye would term same.

As to what body—what has thou abused? What hast thou used? What hast thou applied? What has thou neglected in thy extremes, thy extremities?

These are consciousnesses, these are bodies.

To give them form or shape—you have no word, you have no form in a three-dimensional world or plane of consciousness to give it to one in the seventh—have you?

Hence that's the form—we might say—"Have You?"

What is the form of this in thy consciousness? It rather indicates that everyone is questioned, "Have you?—Have You?"

That might be called the form. It is that which is thy concept of that being asked thyself—not that ye have formed of another.

With that sojourn then the entity finds need for, as it were, the giving expression of same again (the answering of "Have You?") in that sphere of consciousness in which there is a way in and through which one may become aware of the experience, the expression and the manifesting of same in a three-dimensional plane.

Hence the entity was born into the earth under what signs? Pisces, ye say. Yet astrologically from the records, these are some two signs off in thy reckoning.

Then from what is the influence drawn? Not merely because Pisces is accredited with an influence of such a nature, but because it *is!* And the "Have You" becomes then "There Is" or "I Am" in materiality or flesh, or material forces—even as He who has passed this way!

The entity as Bainbridge was born in the English land under the *sign*, as ye would term, of Scorpio; or from Venus as the second influence.

We find that the activity of the same entity in the earthly experience before that, in a French sojourn, followed the entrance into Venus.

What was the life there? How the application?

A child of love! A child of love—the most hopeful of all experiences of any that may come into a material existence; and to some in the earth that most dreaded, that most feared!

(These side remarks become more overburdening than what you are trying to obtain! but you've opened a big subject, haven't you?)

In Venus the body-form is near to that in the three dimensional plane. For it is what may be said to be rather *all*-inclusive! For it is that ye would call love—which, to be sure, may be licentious, selfish; which also may be so large, so inclusive as to take on the less of self and more of the ideal, more of that which is *giving.*

What is love? Then what is Venus? It is beauty, love, hope, charity—yet all of these have their extremes. But these extremes are not in the expressive nature or manner as may be found in that tone or attunement of Uranus; for they (in Venus) are more in the order that they blend as one with another.

So the entity passed through that experience, and on entering into materiality abused same; as the wastrel who sought those expressions of same in the loveliness for self alone, without giving—giving of self in return for same.

Hence we find the influences wielded in the sojourn of the entity from the astrological aspects or emotions of the mental nature are the ruling, yet must be governed by a standard.

And when self is the standard, it becomes very distorted in materiality.

Before that we find the influence was drawn for a universality of activity from Jupiter; in those experiences of the entity's sojourn or activity as the minister or teacher in Lucius. For the entity gave for the gospel's sake, a love, an activity and a hope through things that had become as of a universal nature.

Yet coming into the Roman influence from the earthly sojourn in Troy, we find that the entity through the Jupiterian environment was trained—as we understand—by being tempered to give self from the very universality, the very bigness of those activities in Jupiter.

For the sojourn in Troy was as the soldier, the carrying out of the order given, with a claim for activities pertaining to world affairs—a spreading.

What form, ye ask, did he take? That which may be described as in the circle with the dot, in which there is the turning within ever if ye will know the answer to thy problems; no matter in what stage of thy consciousness ye may be. For "Lo, I meet thee *within* thy holy temple," is the promise.

And the pattern is ever, "have you?" In other words, have you love? or the circle within, and not for self? but that He that giveth power, that meeteth within, may be magnified?

Have you rather abased self that the glory may be magnified that thou didst have with Him before the worlds were, before a division of consciousness came?

These become as it were a part of thy experiences, then, through the astrological sojourns or environs from which all take their turn, their attunement.

And we find that the experience of the entity before that, as Uhjltd [pronounced *ul-t*], was from even without the sphere of thine own orb; for the entity came from those centers about which thine own solar system moves—in Arcturus.

For there had come from those activities, in Uhjltd, the knowledge of the oneness, and of those forces and powers that would set as it were the universality of its relationships, through its unity of purpose in all spheres of human experience; by the entity becoming how? Not aliens, then—not bastards before the Lord—but sons—co-heirs with Him in the Father's kingdom.

Yet the quick return to the earthly sojourn in Troy, and the abuse of these, the turning of these for self—in the activities attempted—brought about the changes that were wrought.

But the entrance into the Ra-Ta experience, when there was the journeying from materiality—or the being translated in materiality as Ra-Ta—was from the infinity forces, or from the Sun; with those influences that draw upon the planet itself, the earth and all those about same.

Is it any wonder that in the ignorance of the earth the activities of that entity were turned into that influence called the sun worshippers? This was because of the abilities of its influences in the experiences of each individual, and the effect upon those things of the earth in nature itself; because of the atmosphere, the forces as they take form from the vapors created even by same; and the very natures or influences upon vegetation!

The very natures or influences from the elemental forces themselves were drawn in those activities of the elements within the earth, that could give off their vibrations because of the influences that attracted or draw away from one another.

This was produced by that which had come into the experiences in materiality, or into being, as the very nature of water with the sun's rays; or the ruler of thy own little solar system, thy own little nature in the form ye may see in the earth!

Hence we find how, as ye draw your patterns from these, that they become a part of the whole. For ye are *relatively* related to all that ye have contacted in materiality, mentality, spirituality! All of these are a portion of thyself in the material plane.

In taking form they become a mental body with its longings for its home, with right and righteousness.

Then that ye know as thy mental self is the form taken, with all of its variations as combined from the things it has been within, without, and in relationship to the activities in materiality as well as in the spheres or various consciousness of "Have you—love, the circle, the Son?"

These become then as the signs of the entity, and ye may draw these from the pattern which has been set. Just as the desert experience, the lines drawn in the temple as represented by the pyramid, the sun, the water, the well, the sea and the ships upon same—because of the very nature of expression—become the *pattern* of the entity in this material plane.

Draw ye then from that which has been shown ye by the paralleling of thy own experiences in the earth. For they each take their form, their symbol, their sound, their color, their stone. For they all bear a relationship one to another, according to what they have done about, "The Lord is in his holy temple, let all the earth keep silent!"

He that would know his own way, his own relationships to Creative Forces or God, may seek through the promises in Him; as set in Jesus of Nazareth—He passeth by! Will ye have Him enter and sup with thee?

Open then thy heart, thy consciousness, for *He* would tarry with thee!

6

Planets

Reading 1650-1

Thus as the soul passes from the aspects about the material environs, or the earth, we find the astrological aspects are represented as stages of consciousness; given names that represent planets or centers, or crystallized activity.

Not that flesh and blood, as known in the earth, dwells therein; but in the consciousness, with the form and manner as befits the environ.

Reading 2620-2

Also during the interims between such [earthly] sojourns, there are consciousnesses, or awarenesses. For, the soul is eternal, it lives on, [it] has a consciousness in the awarenesses of that which has been builded.

Reading 3744-4

. . . it is self, and selfishness, that would damn the individual soul unto one or the other of those forces that bring about the change that must be in those that willfully wrong his Maker. It is not that which man does or leaves undone, but rather that indifference toward the creation [other creatures] that makes or loses for the individual entity. Then, let's be up and doing . . .

Reading 5755-1

For it is not strange that music, color [and] vibration are all a part of the planets, just as the planets are a part—and a pattern—of the whole universe.

Reading 900-16

For, without passing through each and every stage of development, there is not the correct vibration to become one with the Creator . . .

Then, in the many stages of development, throughout the universal, or in the great system of the universal forces, and each stage of development [is] made manifest through flesh, which is the testing portion of the universal vibration. In this manner then, and for this reason, all [are] made manifest in flesh and [there is] development, through the eons of time, space, and [that] *called* eternity.

Reading 281-55

Each planetary influence vibrates at a different rate of vibration. An entity entering that influence enters that vibration; [it is] not necessary that he change, but it is the grace of God that he may! It is part of the universal consciousness, the universal law.

Reading 5755-1

Hence the entity passes along those stages that some have seen as planes, some have seen as steps, some have seen as cycles, and some have experienced as places.

Reading 900-10

In the illustration of this, we find in the man as called Jesus. In this: This man, as man, makes the will the will of the Father, then becoming one with the Father and the model for man . . .

When the soul reached that development in which it reached earth's plane, it became in the flesh the model, as it had reached through the developments in those spheres, or planets, known in [the] earth's plane, obtaining then One in All.

As in Mercury pertaining of Mind. In Mars of Madness [temper, anger, rage]. In Earth as of Flesh. In Venus as Love. In Jupiter as Strength. In

Saturn as the beginning of earthly woes, that to which all insufficient matter is cast for the beginning. In that of Uranus as of the Psychic. In that of Neptune as of Mystic. In Septimus [Pluto?] as of Consciousness. In Arcturus [the star gate] as of the developing.

MERCURY
Reading 1650-1
. . . we find [that] the mental body is both finite and infinite, a part of self and yet a part of a universal consciousness—or the mind of the Maker.

Reading 633-2
Mercury brings the high mental abilities; the faculties that at times may become the developing for the soul or at others turned to the aggrandizement of selfish interests.

For the entity is among those who have entered the earth during those years when there was the great entrance of those who have risen high in their abilities; and who are then passing through those periods when there must be the application of the will, else the very abilities that have been maintained in the Sun and Mercurian influences will become as stumbling-blocks . . .

Reading 3744-2
Mind is the factor that is in direct opposition of will. Mind being that control of, or being the spark of the Maker, the *will*, [that which makes one] the individual when we reach the plane of man.

Reading 115-1
In Mercury the mental influences are abroad, either for the uplifting in the activities of the mental being, or turned into those of selfish natures.

Reading 122-1
. . . the ability of the entity, when the influences of Mercury, especially, are considered, [is] to gain much by what has been and is termed in physical plane as actual experience, and many learn *only* from such.

Reading 228-2

One who, with the Mercury influence then, studies into the mysteries of the mental forces and the action of physical, in the material world, and the action of physical, spiritual and elemental forces in a material world.

Reading 267-1

This benevolent Uranian influence, meted with that arising again from the Mercurian (or Mercury) influence, will give the better ability for the discernment of all these influences of the higher vibration, or the higher influences in the experience of the entity.

Reading 270-15

As in respect then to this entity [270], in entering we find the entity coming under those influences first in Mercury, which gives the ability to reason well as appertains to the material conditions of life.

Reading 272-4

In Mercury we find one of high mental abilities, as indicated by the manner in which the entity—or present body—progressed, and progresses, in the ability to gather in *information* of any character or nature, as indicated in the work in the schools, as indicated in the work in associations with groups or individuals.

Reading 274-1

The Mercurian influence is for a high *mental* ability, as well as an adaptability to the various influences that affect the mental (this being in the broader sense of mental, in the *material*-mental as well as the higher or super forces in its activity) and that are being used through the principles held or maintained by activities of the entity.

VENUS
Reading 1990-3

In the astrological aspects we find that, through influences from sojourns in the Venus environs, the entity is a lover of beauty; especially of song.

And there should be given training . . . [for] the awakening for the entity in those influences . . . for the use of the entity's voice in *praise* and in thanksgiving . . .

Hence all things that have to do with phases of man's ability of expression in beautiful ways and manners will be of interest . . . whether pertaining to nature, to voice or song, or even to art subjects.

Reading 2571-1

As Venus is the ruling influence in the experience, we find that the home will be, should be, the channel through which the greater abilities . . . may be made manifest.

Not that there are not abilities in music, in art . . .

But making an artistic home, making a home that is the expression of beauty in *all* its phases, is the greater career of *any* individual soul. This [the home] is the closer expression of that which has been manifested in the experiences of man's advent into materiality.

Reading 5755-1

In Venus the body-form is near to that [which is] in the three dimensional plane. For it is what may be said to be rather *all*-inclusive! For it is that ye would call love—which, to be sure, may be licentious, selfish; which also may be so large, so inclusive as to take on the less of self and more of the ideal, more of that which is *giving*.

What is love? Then what is Venus? It is beauty, love, hope, charity—yet all of these have their extremes. But these extremes are not in the expressive nature or manner . . . found in that tone or attunement of Uranus [the planet of extremes]; for they (in Venus) are more in the order that they blend one with another.

Reading 238-2

In that in Venus is seen the love of mankind, the love of the fellow man; yet in this same may be found that which, taken contrariwise, will bring hardships that are hard often in the earth's experience, unless judged by that which has been builded within self; for the soul is that portion of the entity that, *being* a portion, or the gift of the Creator or Creative Energy, is builded to be presented to, or made one with, that

Whole. Not that the soul loses its identity in the Whole, but knows itself to be in accord and one *with* same. In making for self selfish interests, or interests that become contrarywise in the law of love, *these* may bring, have brought—as will be seen—some conditions *hard* to be understood.

Reading 243–10

One that is in that position of making friends easily, and just as easily losing same; yet there are friendships made that make for the better understanding in the experience, and in those of *Venus* forces comes the love that is *innate* in the experience of the entity. Through all the vicissitudes of life this remaineth, for the entity has gained much that makes for that as was given—"There is a friend that sticketh closer than a brother," and "he that is just kind to the least of these, my little ones, is greater than he that hath taken a mighty city."

Reading 255–5

In Venus, then—love, beauty; symmetrical forces in the body, the body mind, in the development of those conditions and things about the body; order, and versatility in the order of conditions.

Reading 270–15

As to that influence in Venus, we find this rather the controlling influence—that of love; for, as seen, the body—the entity—may be governed, may be controlled, may be persuaded even to self's *undoing*, in manners, by and through love; yet may never be driven by force, whether of mental or of power; for *under* such the entity finds same irksome, and the desire of *rebellion* comes within the being of the entity, and especially so in the influence of Uranus, which brings high ennobling, good, in the body, yet when others appear not to consider same, then the opposite may be that which the entity seeks to carry out in action. Hence, we find one, without respect of will, that finds many irregular, many absorbing conditions, that apparently are contrary-wise; whether in friendships, whether in business, whether in social relations or in home, that keep—apparently—the whole of self *at times* in turmoil. There *is* a reason for such—for nothing comes by chance, and that of cause and effect is unalterable. Seek the cause. Make the correction.

Prepare the builder—which is *in* the mental, and the application of will as respecting same, and the spirit of that which is impelling throughout life, as it projects itself through the various phases of experience, will bring in the *bodily*—whether mental, physical or material—the results that are in keeping with the expenditure of that given.

Reading 282-2

In Venus, as seen—this as a *ruling* influence—with Mercury, Jupiter *and* Uranus, makes for an extremist in the affairs of the heart or of the head. This also needs to be attuned to an ideal, else the entity may find that when *ideas* have seemed to fail the interest in and the care for conditions that have been even of the head, the heart, or the home, suddenly become as nothing in the entity's experience, unless *ideals* are followed rather than ideas; for with an *ideal* one may reason through the spiritual forces, and not wholly from those of the material circumstances or conditions in the experience or the affairs of a body.

Reading 289-9

In Venus we find the beauty, love, home. These are latent and manifested forces in the experience of the entity. Oft, as will be seen from the material sojourns in the earth, there are those relationships with individuals that would apparently contradict some of those deeper forces. Yet others should see, others should know, God looketh on the heart, not the outward appearances. Oft the entity, then, acts in manners, in relationships, that it the entity does not feel, does not even desire to manifest; and yet it does.

Reading 1193-1

Also in Venus those tendencies that are both good *and* bad are indicated. Love, justice, mercy, patience, endurance; and also self-indulgences, tendencies for neglect, hoping for the loving or patient influence of others that may bear with self.

MARS
Reading 3621-1

Astrologically we find Mars, Mercury, Venus, and Jupiter—and note their importance. [Their order—entity entered from Mars.] Anger may upset the body and cause a great deal of disturbance, to others as well as self.

Be angry but sin not. You will learn it only in patience and in self-possession.

Reading 3416–1

Astrologically we find quite a few variations in the entity's experiences. Besides Mercury, we find Neptune, Saturn, and Mars always stepping in. Hence it has appeared to the entity at times that many of the associates . . . can get mad easier than anybody. Yet the entity may be mad and sin not. Righteous anger is a virtue. He that has no temper is very weak, but he that controls not his temper is much worse. That ye experience . . . at times. This is active patience. Don't think it, much less do it. For as the man thinketh in his heart, so is he.

Reading 1434–1

For the inclinations from the Martian influences are for anger to easily arise in the experiences when the entity is fraught [frustrated] in its activities, in the associations, in its determinations.

And it usually has its way, unless there is reason and love and care and precaution shown by those that direct the developing or formative periods.

Reading 3340–1

In Mars we find this activity. The entity will never be called lazy. May be called stubborn at times, but this, too, may be directed—not by undue punishment but by reasoning with an appealing to the entity . . . Not that there should be a prize for goodness, but remembering that virtue has its own reward, even in those attempting to direct or train children.

Reading 99–6

In the influence seen in Mars, this makes for those of madness, of anger, of wrath, and in the entity's experience those born in June or July do often rile the entity in their relationships one with another. These influences may be changed only by the application of self, individually, to such relationships. Never may the entity act *toward* an individual as they did not exist; never may the entity act *toward* an experience as though it had no part; for the entity's development has been so toward that of the Whole, that all experience, good or bad, must influence the next act, whether mental or material to the entity.

Reading 106–3

In the present, we find, then, one that has been considered as an exceptional one in all conditions pertaining, especially, to those of the mental and of the financial, co-related with the ennobling influences in either, for we find the entity took its flight in the present sphere from that of Mars. Hence the influences as come in the present plane are ever with that resistance, as it were, in the elementals of the entity; elementals meaning attributes of mental, with the ennobling influence of Jupiter and of Mercury, and of Neptune, with adverse forces at times with Venus, and at times good influences from Saturn, and at times very bad. Hence we find many conditions in the past life, as shown in the earth's plane, contradictory one with the other; yet were these studied wholly, we find the greater influence is yielded with the will, and that the entity has that of the combative nature in the present earth's plane.

Reading 280–1

The influences from Mars make one of high temper, one that rages at some very trivial matter; yet things of great import, that would be a worry or disturbing factor to many, the body laughs at or passes over as being a non-essential for worry, or for even disagreements. Yet often does the entity find those experiences where great problems with the minor things cause dissension in the activity of the entity or body in the present.

Reading 289–9

Mars—not as to anger, but as to activity. Not that the entity doesn't get mad—it does! most often at self, however.

Reading 322-2

Also from Mars we find those active influences in those periods where, to the entity, it has meant the representing of the minority activity in relationships with others; and acting in the capacity oft rather as the peacemaker (which would be at-variance, as indicated, to that which would be from the purely astrological aspect).

Not that this indicates there is no temper; nor that the entity does not find at times outlets to express the disagreements with conditions, circumstances, individuals' activities and the like; yet rather does the entity take same—and has taken same—with the air of one who does *accomplish* things, who has accomplished things, even in the trying positions in experiences with the fellow man.

Reading 441-1

The activities also in Mars make for a temperament that is hard to be dealt with, when the entity is in the right in its activities; and often others—that are less sturdy, less well-set in their ideals as to principle or as to activity—consider the actions of the entity as being questionable and as standing in the light of self's best interests. These are of the mental equipment, yet the *mind* is the builder of the activities, even in the material environs.

Reading 1182-1

These then are the astrological forces, that we find are rather unusual. Mars is rather not an adverse influence, not benevolent, but the mystery force or influence in the experiences of the entity.

For Mars represents and is the influence that makes for urges within the innate forces of anger, madness, wrath, strength, [and] endurance. And these then in their more benevolent or expressive ways have brought, will bring, the interesting experiences, provided these are looked upon rather as stepping-stones and helpful experiences than those that make for the shortcomings.

Hindrances should not create in the experience of the entity, then, the expressions from self of indifference or of grudges or of hate; for these are of those influences and forces that wreck, ruin, and bring dissension and strife, and those things that make the heart of men afraid.

JUPITER
Reading 23-1
In Jupiter, gives for the broadness of the vision, and of those that bring to the entity those conditions that make for ennobleness, enlargement of the abilities in the relationships as respecting affluence in the material plane.

Reading 99-6
In the influences seen in Jupiter, makes for that in the entity's experience of gaining a lesson from *every* experience, and with the application of will may the entity *use* such expcrience as a stepping-stone for development of self, as related to the making of self in a closer relationship to the fellow man, thus fulfilling that of divine force or power; for no man may do *for* the Creative Energy, other than lending or aiding the fellow man; for both being a portion *of* the divine, hence may the entity oft be the crutch, or the handle, or the rope to which another may tie, and thus may the entity make *men* of pieces.

Reading 172-3
In Jupiter comes that of the bigness, nobleness, and the broad-mindedness of the entity—and this, varied with the elements as are seen and as has been given, shows how the variations *as* come individually, and to groups and masses.

One, then, that is in the position of meaning much to many.

Reading 189-3
Jupiter has made for not only the high ennobling influence but the tendency for relationships that deal with large numbers of peoples.

Reading 274-1
Jupiter makes for abilities in many varied directions; the associations with a great number of individuals, dealing in principles that are of a basic influence and that tend to make for the larger *ennobling* influences in the experience, or that make up (when classed from the composite sense) the activities of the entity. Or, as may be termed, there is nothing little or underhanded, or superfluous, in the make-up of the entity in its

present experience, as in its dealing with its fellow man or in its activities one with another; making for a *trusting* nature, and the trustworthiness that may be put in the activities of the entity as related to associations with others.

Reading 2869-1

In Venus with Jupiter we see those abilities to appreciate those things and those experiences that are as from the realm of the universal consciousness, as indicated in the song of the bird, the music as of the stream, the beauty as of nature; and yet with Jupiter these become universal forces, or those activities in the material plane will have to do with groups and masses, rather than [with] individuals; though it may be individual in its application.

Reading 1990-3

From the Jupiterian sojourn we find not only the benevolent but the adverse forces. For, while Venus *with* the Jupiterian brings the enjoyment of the beautiful in ways that would pertain to a universal consciousness or activity, the adverse in Mars indicates that wrath . . . may bring those things that will cause the influence to be in a reverse manner . . .

Reading 299-1

In Jupiter, as will be seen, beauty of face, figure, and mind. These will naturally, with the incoming influence, make for one that will be inquisitive, and seeking to know the *reason*, which—while not unusual *ordinarily* in a child or a *developing* one—will be unusual to a marked degree in *this* entity as for *causes*, as well as reason; making, then, those precautions that those who give answers to the seeking and developing mind give those that are an answer *in* Truth as *near* as *is* possible to be done, under any and all circumstance! This, as will be seen, will make for a development that will make apparent one ever *old* for its year, and years, yet the *beauty* in the *abilities* of the entity will repay all that are associated with same in the beauty of the life, in the development of the mental forces, in the *abilities* of the entity in many—or all—directions. Hence nature, nature's activities, should be that as will enable the body, physically, mentally, to ask its questions. Developing in a *moderate* manner the athletic body will aid in its better development in the physical and mental body, and unfoldment also.

Reading 1442-1

As we find . . . those influences in the astrological aspects show Jupiter rather as the ruling force [entity entered from Jupiter].

Hence . . . the entity's activities must have to do with the many . . .

Those influences in Venus make for an open, frank, loving disposition; making for friends in most any walk or every walk of life.

Reading 2890-2

In Jupiter we find the great ennobling influences, the broad-mindedness, the ability to consider others, the universal consciousnesses that are a part of the entity's unfoldment.

We find in Venus that unusual attraction that the opposite sex will have for the entity, and the entity for the opposite sex. Hence those relationships in such should be the problems as well as the studies and the guidance through the periods especially in the next cycle—or during the next seven years for the entity.

In Mercury and in Mars we find the energetic activities of mind and of body, and at times . . . appearing expressive in the experience of others as related to the entity as a meddler. Yet these are the benevolent forces, if those activities . . . of the entity are used and analyzed in that way of aiding the entity in its preparations through such experiences.

Reading 1206-3

In Jupiter we find the associations making for those tendencies for large groups . . . in relationships with the entity. This makes also for those inclinations that . . . will be great amounts of this world's goods [in the entity's experiences]. May the training also then not only in its teen age [years] but throughout its developments be as to the use of same [wealth], as being lent from Creative Forces and energies and not . . . for . . . self-indulgence . . .

SATURN
Reading 1981–1

In Saturn we find the sudden or violent changes—those influences and environs that do not grow, as it were, but are sudden by that of change of circumstance, materially, or by activities apparently upon the part of others that become a part of self in the very associations. And yet these are testing periods of thy endurance, of thy patience, of thy love of truth, harmony and the spirit that faileth not.

From the combination of this with Uranus we find the extremes; the environs materially or mentally in which the very opposites may be expected. Remember, only in Christ, Jesus, do extremes meet.

Reading 361–4

From Saturn we find the tendency for the starting of new experiences . . . new associations . . . and unless these are tempered with the mental influences they are rarely carried to their full termination. This again would be as a warning . . . When thou hast chosen that direction, that activity thou would take, know that thou art kept in a balance that is of the material, mental and spiritual influences near to right. Then lay it not aside until it, the activity, has borne fruit in thine mental and material experience.

Reading 324–5

The influences in Mars and Saturn show for urges that will develop towards those things pertaining to music, unusual things, and will be continually starting this or that activity which has to do or deals with new associations, new relations, new activities . . . of not only self but those about the entity.

Reading 3205–1

We find in Saturn many changes in the experience. The entity will ever find itself very opposed to being poor, and would go to almost any length to obtain the material things of life. Let not these, thy good works, be evil spoken of because of material things being considered to such a degree as to disregard others' privileges or obligations.

Reading 1426-1

In Saturn we find the inclinations for changes, as to this, that or the other; and to muddle a great many things together in the activity.

Hence that injunction as given by the sages of old, "The merchant is never the student; neither is the student ever the merchant," should be . . . a part of the entity's program in its choice of its activity in this experience.

Reading 3806-1

Astrologically we find that Venus, Saturn and Neptune are the urges. Thus these will be found to make many changes, yet the entity is one loving, a friend, one who may be counted on as a friend, or as a foe, to be sincere—if the directions are given properly for the entity through these trying periods.

Reading 1431-1

In the astrological activities that produce . . . these experiences [desire for travel, desire for change] as innate, we find Uranus, Neptune, Saturn as ruling influences; which make for interest in yet the fear of occult and mystic forces. But rather if there is . . . the expression of the *psychic*, rather than occult *or* mystic, we may find greater development, greater experiences for the entity.

For in Uranus we find the extremes, and when the entity is very good, it's very, *very* good . . .

Those then of the experience must be tempered . . . with . . . the Venus influence.

While the Venus influences are latent, these should find the greater expression; else the urges as from Saturn would make for the entity having *many* homes, or many marriages . . .

For consistency and persistency are the sisters of patience; patience the entity needs to learn as its lesson in this experience.

Reading 945-1

For the earth and Saturn are opposites, as it were . . . to Saturn go those that would renew or begin again, or who have blotted from their experience much that may be set in motion again through other influences and environs that have been a portion of the entity's experience.

URANUS
Reading 1206-3
From the Uranian influences we find the extremist. And these tendencies . . . will develop especially through the early teen age years, when there will be moods and . . . wonderments . . . These [Uranian tendencies] make for also the intuitive influences and the abilities for the development in the very psychic forces of the entity.

Reading 2572-1
In the urges from astrological aspects we find Mercury, Uranus, Venus and Jupiter as the influences through which the entity has received an awareness.

One of the high mental ability, yet one very extreme in many ways.

Oft . . . too easily discouraged. Hence . . . it will require that the entity set a purpose and a goal, and be not deterred from same . . .

Reading 38-1
Those of exceptional abilities with Uranian influence may be *well* said also to mean exceptional abilities to err, or to be led astray in the direction not best for . . . self's development.

Reading 2571-1
In Uranus we find the extremes, and the interest in the occult—or the mystical. This is well, if it is balanced in the spiritual nature . . .

Reading 1911-1
In . . . benevolent influences in Mars and Uranus [both in Libra, sign of balance], these bring for the exceptional abilities as respecting intuitive forces for the body, and as for the abilities . . . to quiet those who would show wrath, or any unkindly feeling toward another. Oft will the entity—if trained, especially in this formative period—be able to act as oil upon troubled waters, as that inter-between which will make for beauty in the lives of those the entity contacts, making for a bond of sympathy, of union, that will be exceptional . . . as well as . . . awakening

of abilities within self . . . that may be the peacemaker, not only among individuals but in groups, in classes, in States, in masses. [Entity entered from Jupiter, with Venus, Mars, and Uranus also influencing.]

Reading 143-1

This entity, we find, took its flight, or position, from the planet of Uranus, with Venus and Mercury controlling the destiny in the present earth's plane. Hence the necessity of the entity's training, especially, in those elements having to do with purity in love and affection, and of nobleness and of goodness . . . that comes with that mode of expressing itself . . . for with the entity under these influences, with the exceptional conditions as come from influences of Uranus, we find [that] the entity's manifestations in the present plane will be exceptionally good or very bad.

Reading 1958-1

It [the entity] is not only a Uranian but an Atlantean, and the combination will be something to *deal with!* as to temper, as to having its way; for it *will* have its way, irrespective, for the first fourteen years . . .

As for the aspects in the Uranian influence, we find the extremes. The entity will be at times very beautiful in character—at others very ugly; very beautiful in body and mind—at others the other extreme. For these will have an influence, and the entity will be an extremist through the first fourteen years of its experience . . .

High mental abilities. One that will make a study of how to have its way . . . *do no*t break the will . . . rather give the lesson by precept and example.

Reading 2005-1

In the Uranian influence we will find the extremes . . .

For there will be periods . . . with a Uranian, when for a few hours or a few minutes or a few days it will be very, very morose . . . These will arise . . . out of nowhere . . .

Reading 5-2

Astrological, then, we find the entity coming under the influence of

Mercury, Jupiter, Saturn, Venus, and Uranus . . .

In . . . the Uranian [influences] . . . periods when there seems to be every condition imaginable awry—whether business relations, social relations, financial conditions—*every* condition seems to be awry. Again there are seasons of, most things come too easy.

Reading 3706-2

In Uranus we find the extremes. Thus the entity in spiritual, in mental and in material things finds periods when it is as to the mountain tops and again in the depths of despair.

Reading 2922-1

Easily might the entity become one that would talk of self too much.

While the entity will ever be a good listener, do direct the entity so that there is always the consideration for others.

Astrologically—we find Uranus (the extremist, of course, in same) . . .

Reading 311-2

. . . know that each thought, each act, is that being builded . . . in their sojourns in the spheres—make for this entering in. As in earth . . . matter takes all its various forms of presentation of . . . energy, *or* force, as radiated from the various effects of this solar aspect . . . all force in *this* [earth] sphere taking on that appearance . . . known as threefold, or the aspects of a threefold nature. As in Jupiter—taking on those ennobling forces, whether they be from earth, from Venus, from Mercury, from Mars . . . As in Saturn—that [sphere] to whom all insufficient matter is cast for its remolding . . . either re-entering through those of the Uranian—which makes for the accentuations of very good or very bad, and making, in their relationships . . . for *extraordinary* conditions; taking on those forces known in earth's plane as from occult influences.

Reading 2443-1

We find in Uranus the extremes, because of an *inner* feeling; and not merely because of the age or of changes . . . in the material environs of the entity. For, we find periods when apparently without reason outwardly there is the overenjoyment . . . and then others when it becomes

rather the recluse, or morose, or . . . inclined to "sulk," as called by some
. . .

Make thy life . . . the well-rounded life; preparing self for the home
rather than for a career. For, the greatest career of *any* individual is to
make a home in such a . . . manner that each occupant—yea, each visitor
to same—is better for having known and come into contact with the
entity.

Reading 1735-2

. . . while the body mental may be termed the *exceptional* in mental
abilities, these should be guided in the proper channels and kept as of a
unit of [the] whole expression; knowing that to sidetrack, to accentuate,
any one portion of experiences in the mental or physical forces of the
body is to prevent the well rounded development as is necessary for . .
. development in the material plane . . .

Keep thine heart pure, thine body strong, thine mind open. Attune
thine inner man to the harps and the chords of the universe, and harken
to the love that brings service—service—to all.

NEPTUNE
Reading 2553-8

. . . the soul and spirit took its flight . . . from that far away force as
exercised in Neptune. Hence we have an entity that . . . will be peculiar
to other people, rarely ever being understood; yet one with the spiritual
insight of the developing in [the] earth plane, and one whom others
would be, could be, benefited by, by being in contact with this entity.

Reading 2308-1

For the extremes of Uranus as well as Neptune are a portion of the
entity's experience . . .

From Neptune we find that being close to waters, on waters, or about
waters, is very well . . . and this also gives those abilities as the mystic—
the interest in the unusual, as in the abilities of seeing, feeling, experi-
encing that which to most would be the unseen forces about the entity.

These are well to be cultivated, not abused, nor encouraged by giving thought to what the reaction should be, but keep the spiritual im-

port, the spiritual necessity—which has been a portion of the entity's experience through one of its sojourns, as one who accepted the veil.

Reading 406-1

Neptune *and* Uranus make for an interest in reading matter that is of an unusual nature. Things that pertain to mysteries, or conditions in individuals' or groups' lives that are unusual, the uncanny and such . . .

And, for the better development of the entity, as it develops or progresses through the experiences of this sojourn, the dwelling near large bodies of water, or upon large bodies of water, will be the natural elements for the development; giving rise to the abilities both in the occult and in the mystic influences.

Reading 2213-1

. . . the conditions as are exhibited in the present earth's plane in . . . love of the sea (see the body has gone to sea).

In the influence then, we find one of many exceptional abilities.

One that is considered eccentric and peculiar, having many change-able moods.

One loving mystery, and every condition as regards . . . a mystery of the sea, and of the sleuth or detective nature.

One that should have been guided close in the study of those things pertaining to the mystery and the occult.

One who will find the . . . greatest abilities in the present earth's plane in the study of the occult forces.

Reading 1426-1

In Neptune we find the inclinations for things that have to do with water and over water and to be on waters . . . These then give an urge again, as through Saturn, for change of scene and change of environ-ment—and the desire for travel . . . those things that are exciting . . . that pertain to the heroic and hero worship. This urge must ever be tem-pered, then, with directing the entity to the character of ideals . . .

Reading 2005-1

Here we find unusual conditions, especially owing to the long periods of interims between material sojourns. And thus . . . one that oft appears to be lost in confusions of itself; being highly sensitive to those influences from without.

Thus . . . an entity whose psychic abilities—if they are developed—may surpass much of that which has been the experience of many . . .

Hence the needs for the study, the directing, the instructing of the entity in the sources of spiritual (not spiritualistic, but spiritual) influences . . .

In the astrological aspects we find Neptune, Uranus, Venus and Saturn as the greater influence . . . Hence we will find the inclination for seeking the unusual places, strange conditions—taking up with and associating with strange surroundings, having strange playmates—the desire for [the] unusual in pets . . .

From the Neptune influences—keep away from large bodies of water! These are opposite from much of that accredited as an influence from the astrological aspects of Neptune; though those things that come *from* and *over* large bodies of water . . . will be of a great interest to the entity; and the knowledge of same should be a part of the entity's experience.

Reading 4228-1

We find the soul and spirit entity took its flight, or its force being present and bringing this present entity's completeness, from . . . Venus' forces, with those of Jupiter, Mercury, Neptune being the ones in the assistance to the conditions bringing the forces to this present plane's development, with afflictions of those in Mars and in that of Septimus. Arcturus being in the greater force for this development upon this plane, [the soul] receiving then the greater force by the influence of Arcturus, with . . . the dwelling forces of Neptune. The Moon's forces being those that have brought, and will bring, many of the influences from the forces of Venus . . .

As these, we find those inclinations:

With the Strength of Jupiter forces, with that of Venus and Neptune . . . one given to letters, and of high exalted positions of self and all concerned therewith. Given to make show, or display, of that element that gives the greater expression of self. Hence, will must be directed, else with the influence of Venus' forces [it] would give detrimental elements in the life.

One whose forces from . . . Mercury will turn in the middle portion of life to those elements pertaining to the chemical forces, with that of Arcturus' forces giving strength to the elements as is directed in the entity.

PLUTO
Reading 3126-1

Astrologically we find most all, in varied spheres, reacting through the soul-consciousness of the entity; Mercury, Pluto, Mars, Venus, Jupiter, Saturn, Neptune. All of these in various manners.

Sudden changes are indicated in Saturn; high mental ability and capabilities in Mercury; self-centeredness in Pluto, and earthward in the application of self. [*Pluto is in Gemini;* author's italics.]

In Venus we find the attraction to and from the opposite sex; in Jupiter a universal consciousness; in Neptune an interest in psychological and spiritual things.

We find in Mars a high, exalted opinion of self; which is well, but abused—as it may be in Pluto, or in Mercury—may become a stumbling-stone rather than a stepping-stone to advancement in this present sojourn.

Reading 583-1

In the relation to those of the planets that has, that is and that will influence this body, we find the strongest of these at the moment of the birth . . . Venus and Neptune were the ruling forces for this body, with that of Mars in the 9th house, of Jupiter in the 12th house, of Uranus in the 7th house, see? Septimus almost at its zenith, yet not the ruling factor in this body's actions on this present plane, for with the position of Venus and Neptune this, the influence of Septimus, [Cayce's name for Pluto] has become changed by the position of Pisces and the constellation of that of Castor and Apollo . . .

One well gifted towards the arts, especially in that of writing, or of composition, or of imagination, or of that that has to do with the finer things of life, as would be through the position [of] Castor, Apollo, Venus and Neptune.

One . . . [who] should be nearer the great waters for its best development . . . will be well for this body to be wary of that of the influence of Septimus and the conjunction that will be within the next six months, else . . . accident, either through self or from the conditions of the trunk or the torso of the body . . .

Reading 1100-27

(Q) *Just what are the effects of Pluto, in conjunction with one's ascendant?*

(A) This as we find is entirely amiss from what we might call a physical expression—but, as we find indicated, these [influences] are a development that is occurring in the universe, or environs about the earth—Pluto. Not as some have indicated that it is gradually being dissipated. It is gradually *growing*, and thus is one of those influences that are to be as a demonstrative activity in the future affairs or developments of man towards the spiritual-minded influences, or those influences outside of himself.

These [individuals] in the present, as might be said, are merely . . . [those] becoming *aware* of same. Rather within the next hundred to two hundred years there may be a great deal of influence [of Pluto] upon the ascendancy of man; for it's closest of those to the activities of the earth, to be sure, and is a *developing* influence, and not one already established.

MOON
Reading 900-14

(Q) *Are there particular times when Moon's influences are particularly strong, and thereby counteract the good influences of Jupiter and Neptune, to bring worldly goods to body's possession? How may he use will to avoid these adverse influences?*

(A) In Moon's influence in this entity has particularly to do with the earthly satisfaction of desire toward opposite sex, in the present plane's sphere. These we find are at times adverse to ennobling forces, and may be made to appear in self to coincide with mysteries of life; using will then to know that each and every such condition must be brought under those forces of Jupiter and Neptune, that this influence, through will, will be turned into that which will bring the better conditions in the life's plane. For with the mental carrying such conditions of any intrigue against ennobling influence in [the] earth's plane, or carrying such intrigue that bring the mysteries of life to naught, these we see work condemnation rather than blessings in the life of an entity. Hence the warnings as given of the Moon's influence at times [in the entity's condition] in earth's plane. Will used directly. Warding against such conditions becoming detrimental to the body's development.

Reading 2459-1

From the Moon we find the tendencies towards the love of the social life, which might easily become a failing—because of its greater abilities as an individual. For, as indicated, the entity's personality will stand out in groups and among its associates in such a manner that all will seek companionship with the entity.

Thus, as given, there are the needs for stressing that latent force in the entity's abilities to judge time, duty, obligation, more than the material things or money.

Reading 3089-1

In Mercury, Venus, Jupiter and Uranus we find the greater activities. The Moon is only a portion of the experience, but it gives the greater emotion.

Reading 2855-1

In coming into the earth's plane in the present, we find . . . the Moon being in that adverse condition, we find the entity has found that there are apparently periods in which everything (as would be termed in earthly parlance) is lucky that the entity touches; other periods wherein everything "goes to pot" that the entity has anything to do with. These are especially as pertaining to investments, and if the entity were to take the time he will find these are those of any conditions that have to do with pleasure seeking in the evenings. These have been failures. The influences rather then are that, at certain periods when Moon is at variance with the various elements that enter from the astrological viewpoint into the life, the entity tends toward investments of that nature.

Will's force and more of that *ennobling*, rather than that of obtaining dollars for the pound of flesh, or irrespective of the result that is to come to other hands.

SUN
Reading 254-2
The strongest power in the destiny of man is the Sun, first; then the closer planets, or those that are coming in ascendency at the time of the birth of the individual—but let it be understood here, no action of any planet or any of the phases of the Sun, Moon, or any of the heavenly bodies surpass the rule of Man's individual will power—the power given by the Creator of man in the beginning, when he became a living soul, with the power of choosing for himself.

Reading 1724-4
The sun is a great influence in the experience of the entity.

Hence the more the entity will find himself associated with those influences or forces that direct the activities or the policies of great undertakings, the better will be the environ for the entity, and greater may there be an expression of the abilities of the entity in all of its phases.

Reading 5746-1
The sun indicates strength and life, while the moon indicates change . . .

Reading 2990-2
Being under those influences of Moon and Sun also, we find in the Sun the strength and in the Moon the weakness.

7

●

Stars, Constellations and Signs

The Star Arcturus
The Star Gate to and from Our Solar System

Editor's Note: According to Edgar Cayce's readings, our solar system is a collective region of soul growth. The Sun and planets are like specialized colleges within a university—the system being the university, and each planet being a specialized college. The entrance into this system is the star Arcturus in the constellation Boötes (the herdsman or plowman). It is the third brightest star in the sky.

Reading 2823-1

Not that the sun that is the center of this solar system is all there is. For the entity has attained to that realm even of Arcturus, or that center from which there may be the entrance into other realms of consciousness. And the entity has chosen in itself to return to the earth for a definite mission.

Reading 5749-14

. . . Arcturus is that which may be called the center of this universe, through which individuals pass and at which period there comes the choice of the individual as to whether it is to return to complete . . . in this planetary system, our sun, the earth sun and its planetary system—or to pass on to others.

Reading 263–15

For Arcturus is that junction between the spheres of activity as related to cosmic force . . . As those influences indicated in Atlantis were as a beginning, so Arcturus in the present might be termed as a beginning.

Constellations and Signs

Editor's Note: Edgar Cayce gave information on the signs of the zodiac as he was contacted for readings; in some cases, he did not have much to say about a particular sign because few people under the influence of that sign requested readings. The best example is Virgo, in which there are only 4 readings mentioning this sign out of over 14,000 total readings! Conversely, he had many people born with their Sun in Aries and Aquarius, resulting in many readings for these signs, of which we have selected a few.

ARIES
Reading 276–2

In entering, we find the influences astrologically in Aries—which will require in the present experience the use of the mental abilities of the entity in making its choice. Hence the particular reference that should be taken as respecting the influences to the entity through the formative period of the mental developments being especially susceptible, that the basis of thought is well founded, or grounded, should be the thing *most* to be considered by those who are responsible for this period.

Reading 279–4

In Aries and Uranus makes for those of tendencies of being easily influenced by suggestion, yet often termed by associates as very hard-headed and set in ways . . .

As in Neptune, with Uranus and Aries influence, will make for those influences that waters, and those of mystic forces, or occult influences, will ever have (as in suggestion) an *influence* in the experience of the body. Allowing self to become subject to, rather than dominating the influences or suggestion, would make the entity a subject of, rather than being able to subject that as is not useful and using that which may be dominated, or to *dominate* that which is harmful in the experience of the entity.

Reading 340-15

One that may be termed by many as being headstrong, and of self's own will; yet much of this has been tempered in the present experience, and reason—or that of the Mercurian influence—has manifested itself in the present experience. This makes for those also of the mental abilities, aptitude in various manners as pertaining to associations, as pertaining to *conditions* in which the entity finds self—in the social relations, in the marital relations, in filial relations. These also are tempered in that of the Aries—or the mind of its own—as respecting such.

Reading 406-1

Through Aries associations, there are the abilities of a high *mental* development; yet there are rather those warnings for this entity regarding accidents to the head. Injuries of some nature may come in the experience of the entity, either during the next four months or early portion of '34. These warnings are from influences that come from Aries or head associations with Mars.

Reading 436-2

As in passing from Pisces into Aries, there are those influences innately and manifested in the mental forces of the body; much of both of these, and they become conflicting in the experience at times of the entity.

Pisces brings rather the mystery and creative forces, and magnanimous aspects in students of—or in the thought of influences in the active principles of individual impulse; with Aries bringing reason, or air, or airy actions, yet reason, more than Pisces would make the demands in the self at times for reasons for every manifestation, whether material conditions, mental or spiritual conditions in the experience of the entity. And at other periods it may be said that the entity becomes rather susceptible to influences about the body, without considering seriously the sources of the information and as to whether same is able to be verified by others or not. Feelings of same impress the entity from this astrological influence, which—as we see—does not only control earth's sojourn but the position of the entity in this sojourn through the planetary influences in the earth's solar system.

Reading 437–2

In the astrological aspects, Aries and Aquarius both. Hence the entity will always do best with associations of those that live near large bodies of water, or who reside across—or have recently crossed—large bodies of water. The entity will continue through the experience to be combative in mental aspects of *personal* experience, as well as others with whom the entity is associated. We will find, however, that beginning at least in the present year—and particularly through those periods of April, or March the 18th to May the 5th—there will be those periods when the influences of occult, or mystic *and* occult, will play an important part in the experiences of the entity in the present sphere. As to how *great* an influence will be the manner of application of will, or of the entity's *using* those influences or being combative with or disregarding those influences, *with* the manifestations of the self's will.

Readings 462–2

In Aries—an entity that uses the head and the mental abilities, rather than the brawn or physical exertions, to accomplish that as would bring those returns for self in any material affairs. Naturally, the mental is builded likewise.

Reading 517–1

As is generally termed, while the entity under Aries makes for one headstrong, head-willed, not always in the present experience has the entity applied in the sojourn that known respecting the laws of the universality of constructive or God force in its experience. Yet these, as we find, have been and are in the expressions of the entity . . .

Reading 621-1

In the first, then, coming under the influence of those two influences known as Pisces and Aries, we have a headstrong individual or mind, as well as one that—when over influenced—becomes somewhat sullen. And if the spirit is broken, or if there is the forcing of the issues with such an individual by those in authority or in power, it may bring about very detrimental influences. Not that the entity is to be left to "run wild," as it were, with its own imaginations or own emotions, yet these are to be used as the influences in a constructive manner. For in the Martian as well as in the Mercurian (and both are in the influence of the mental body) these are to be used as judgements, and as the application in the experience of the entity, to reason with. For naturally, of nature itself, each soul seeks for the expression of that which is built within self as related to *creative* influences either from the objective or the egotistical; for these are as the positive and negative forces in the experience of every soul in its activity in the earth—objective as positive and egotistical as negative influences. If the appeal comes to the entity (or in a developing mind) such that what is done is for the exaltation of self, more and more egotism and less and less initiative is there to be seen in the activity of the soul. If what is done is more and more of the positive nature, that the good may arise from those influences though they may appear to be of the personal nature, more and more are the positive forces developed and more and more universal is the aid that the individual or soul may give to its surroundings, and more and more it may gather from same.

Readings 1462-1

In this entity's experience then from the astrological aspects (*mental* urges from sojourns from without the material plane, as indicated above), we find these become as the heady; or Aries . . .

Reading 2124-3

One, as in Aries, that has a mind of his own, and expresses same at times to where some would call the entity tending towards hardheaded, or a man of his own mind. This has been altered much by the application of will as respecting same . . .

TAURUS
Reading 1159-1
. . . Taurus [makes one] rather headstrong . . .

Reading 2790-2
In the constellations, we find under Taurus, which gives, with the afflictions of Mercury, those tendencies towards those portions in the physical for afflictions in the body. With the forces of Jupiter and Venus [the planet that rules Taurus], these may be overcome, even irrespective of will upon certain days, and these appear in the sphere of the destiny as controlled by the forces in the planets . . .

Reading 2484-1
In taking the position in the present earth plane, we find the entity comes under the influence of Pisces and of Taurus [both ruled by Venus]. Hence, we find a condition that is almost combative in the personality of the entity, as is exhibited in the present earth's plane . . .

As given, one that appears often to others as not wholly meaning what is said, in action or in word; yet only not understood, for the entity, with the influence of the Jupiterian forces, is one that is staid in self, and the satisfaction of knowing that self is right, irrespective of the ideas, thoughts or opinion of others, goes in that direction often to the entity's own undoing, in the minor things in life.

One that has an ennobling influence in the lives of many; also bringing to others those influences that may lead to that which is unstable; for, as given, the entity is often misunderstood.

In the conditions, then, as bring the best influence in the life of the entity, we find that in the next two years will be the greatest influence in the life, in the present earth's plane . . .

Editor's Note: The following is a drawing guided by Cayce and includes an image of the sign and a description. It is part of a Life Seal that Cayce said would help the soul.

Reading 538-72
. . . the central figure, or the larger, would be the goddess Isis, *with*

Horus upon the lap; this indicating especially the body of the goddess with the headdress, to be sure, of Taurus, or in that form, with the figure of the sun as the symbol in or between the horns of same. All of this would be in bronze color, save the center sun symbol which would be white. Indicate the special significance to Horus in the heart, or the manner of the entity's development towards children, motherhood, and the activities.

Reading 1641-1

As to the astrological aspects, these we find not so much because of the position of a star or planet, or a zodiacal sign; though these as we will find are in the experience of the entity rather those that run true to activities in which there will occur much that would be in keeping with that often accredited to astrological aspects.

For both Taurus *and* Aquarius make for an influence. Thus we will find these will be a part of the experience, but according to what the entity does about the influence:

Inquisitive—yes; and at times to its own confusion it may be.

A very set and determined manner, yes—at times to its own activity for the more perfect material and mental comprehension of that as may be in mind or the intent and purpose of the entity.

GEMINI
Reading 195-8

We find that the greater influence comes from that of Mercury and Saturn, both being in the birth sign Gemini at the period of birth, but Saturn in that position of the square with Jupiter and Venus. This we find brings many conditions that in the thoughts of others make the appearance of this individual's way of thinking peculiar.

One given to be especially given to the ideas relating to inventions and the development of each that would bring the better conditions to the lives of his fellow man.

One that will find the inclination to be of assistance to many peoples, and will also find many losses, financially, in such conditions, yet building continually in self through such transactions, if the body will but will itself to build upon such conditions.

Editor's Note: The following is a drawing guided by Cayce and includes an image of the sign and a description. It is part of a Life Seal that Cayce said would help the soul.

Reading 294-206

. . . indicate a mountain, and the symbol or sign that is the symbol of Gemini—or the two-bodied figure, or united bodies as a figure (small), on the edge of this mountain. The vegetation here would be very verdant, in the central portion; this shading off to the left in that as of the temple—or the crystal, or an obelisk with the crystal in the top. This, to be sure, would not be too large a figure; with many figures at worship about the light that comes from this obelisk.

CANCER
Reading 304-5

With the zodiacal signs and influences in that of Cancer, the influences of the Mars and Uranus forces have brought many sudden changes to structural conditions in the physical body. These have been at times beneficial to development, again to the detriment—because of the lack of the exercising of will in the correct or direct manner, and the selfish forces in that of desire being the factor or appetite to be met with, and these have brought many conditions that must again be met and overcome in earth's plane. [GD's note: Mr. [304] had been a drunkard for many years during first half of his life; his wife and children had suffered for it.]

As to the influences then, we find these conditions:

One that has had many bodily physical influences exercised in the life. [GD's note: His children told me that nearly every bone in his body had been broken at one time or another.]

One that overcomes all of the forces from the material world, for with Venus forces giving the ultra influence in the sign with Uranus experiences brings the overcoming of much when will is exercised to the degree that the answering of the spirit and soul forces with the call of the inner man comes to the *I Am.*

In the influence of Mercury with Venus in Cancer brings the higher mental attributes to the physical, and with the will might and may be exercised to the degree to make the entity the leader among many classes and over the masses of men, yet as an individual standing with the minority. In the element of Venus has brought and does bring many cares in the field of affection, and has brought many of the earthly ills and the material cares and worry. Exercise will that these may be used as development and not meted against that karma that is made in each entity's sojourn in the earth's plane.

This we find then one that would be well in any vocation where the classes and masses are the ruling factor rather than of individual effort in production alone. In the elements or forces that have to do with Mercury's influence in earth plane especially. In the force then of that as a producer in field or stream or wood, or in that as the producer for that which when developed in the mental forces of the classes and masses will find fruitage, and will bring forth many manifold increases.

In the forces then as shown in this entity's sojourn here, as weighed with the will, we find these:

There has been much made in the sojourn here to be met and over-come. There has been development in the mental and the ultra forces, for in the present these we find the influence of those in Cancer's con-stellation with Uranus in its present position with earth's sphere, that those in Venus that do not allow the love or the element of the carnal to enter in the life may bring forth fruit worthy of acceptance before Him who giveth all things.

In the will's influence then, let those that would, beware of these conditions, else in the bodily forces of the physical will be created that which will be the destructive element in earth plane.

Reading 1910–1

In the astrological influences, then, these are seen as innate:

Coming under the astrological influence of Cancer and Capricorn, these have little save as passing fancies of interest; yet under Venus *with* same, those inductive influences of various forms of music, chants, odors, and such, weave for the entity a mysterious force as is oft felt as would like to indulge *in* without knowing its full meaning; for, as the entity will—and does—experience, to the entity—and to all, as a warn-ing—mysticism oft, under such influence, bespeaks carnal sensuousness, but *under* the same influence—in an occult establishment of *vision*—becomes stabilizing in its effect upon the abilities, to make *conscious* images of an unseen force. Well that this differentiation be studied and considered well, *especially* by *this* entity, would the entity become *stabilized* in the developments for self as respecting the mysteries of life and the influences occidental and oriental life has upon same.

In the same influence is seen that felt exercised in the entity's experience in Neptune and Venus, in how that the *mysteries* of the deep (such as indulged in, in the visions as are brought up, or to the entity, either in the characterization of the literature the entity seeks or the visions as are had by entity) bespeak of creative forces to the entity, but are often turned into the mysteries of formality, or formalism. Do not misjudge or misinterpret these experiences or influences in the entity's experience.

In those conditions as make for the studies of the entity, the seeking—as innate forces—for the influences held by those who concentrate in the silence and in the mental imaginative forces—these, guided by a stabilized *ideal*, may be made most helpful; these—run rampant, without consideration as to whether same becomes riotous in activity; not clothed, to be sure, in any form of censure, but as to whether same becomes a continuity of influences as of helpfulness or riotousness—without respect of persons, places or things—is different.

In the influences as seen that the entity holds upon individuals and associations as related to environments and hereditary influences, these are as hedged BY the entity's experience—as will be seen through those influences acted upon by the will of the entity in the various experiences. This also makes for that tendency of becoming ofttimes the recluse—that is, in self's actions and activities—when more of a general and mediocre condition would be the most *enlightening* and helpful. At other times it is found that the entity is too quick spoken, too outspoken in the expression as to try *out* others, when proper consideration of *their* place, time and condition is not given by the entity, in relationship to the individual's development as to environment or hereditary influence. Hereditary influence and environment here mean rather as of that *innately* builded, than physically manifested.

In the influences of likes and dislikes in the entity, here we find these become very decided all of a sudden and as much of a sudden they change. This is a characterization of those whose influences are under Neptune or Cancer, with the days in that period, in that sphere in which the entity finds expression, or entering in, coming in, near the dog days. Then, as to animals and their relationships—these are held too close to as of one. All *force* and all *power* is of one source, as is life—but the *associations* of each are individual, and should be classified so *by* the entity in its *study* of the relationships of animal, matter, celestial matter, material matter. In *spirit* one, but all flesh is not of one flesh—as some are given a cosmic influence only and others the ability to become one with the creative energy itself, in its *cleansing* of itself to be one in its relationships.

In the influences seen in those of the arts, these—when they take on the mysterious forces—are of interest; so, then, the futuristic views become interesting and mean much to the entity, when to others little is seen. This may be made extreme or worthwhile in the entity's experience.

LEO
Reading 2905-3

As will be found, Leo—or the consciousness of that mind will be a part of the entity's awareness. Thus at times the entity will appear headstrong, willful; yet, as has been indicated, there are other influences of the benevolent nature (from Jupiter) making for the broadness, the bigness of the entity's abilities. In Venus combined with same, we find a great deal of color, a great deal of emotion, will be a part of the entity's experience.

Music, then, should play an important part in the experience of the entity in the earth; through same coming some of the great moments of individual experience of the entity in the contacts made in the feeling of the heart, the mind, the body—the rhythm of same that gives to the body its activity, its vivaciousness, the beauty of rhythm.

All of these should and will be parts of the entity's experience, if it lives its normal experience. These tempered with mercy, judgment, and the law of love, will become beautiful. These environed with hate or jealousy will become detrimental to the better well being. For, as indicated do not break the entity's will; for, it will be a headstrong individual. Then by reason, by kindness, by patience, by persistence, by loving, the entity may be lead into the ways in which there may be the greater expression of Jupiter and Venus, as well as Mars and Mercury in this particular sojourn.

The activities of the entity should be in those fields pertaining to literary activities; pertaining, those things having to do with rhythm of the body or the mind, in verse in song. In these the entity may give expression to its greater feelings.

Then these should be as hobbies as parts of the entity's life. For the home may, to the entity become the great part of its career, of its discovery of love and hope and beauty, and those things that bring about peace and harmony into the souls of individuals.

Reading 3791-1

In the present plane, we find the entity comes from those conditions or places of Venus. And while the zodiacal conditions play some part in the present plane, these are very little when compared to the influence of other conditions that appear from force of the entity's sojourn in other spheres. The entity, we find, was completed in the afternoon of this day and with the influence of Venus, Mercury, Uranus and Mars when at the better aspect of Jupiter. Yet adverse influence when Mars is at the square of Saturn. Moon's influence being good when sun's influence comes with Leo, the birth sign, and with the sign of the Jupiter's forces in Leo.

Then we have these inclinations in the present earth's plane irrespective of wills:

One who is of a very determined nature.

One who mounts many obstacles when the mental has the incentive for good.

One that loves the beautiful in every form and manner.

One that is attracted to children especially and gives and shows much filial love for young children.

One that is very ambitious for self and is particularly adaptable to the present line of endeavor.

One that will reach the greater heights in the chosen profession near the age of 52.

One who could, with will, have made of himself, an excellent physician.

One who studies much of occult forces and of mysticism, of theological surveys in strange tongues.

One that feels the innate force ever present and only feels the need of the awakening to be in greater position.

One who mounts many obstacles through the occult forces latent in self.

One who would go far in the study of psychological and psychic problems.

One who will rule many by the love manifest in self towards others.

One that finds the greater joy in giving joy to others.

One that should take care that it does not become selfish or dictatorial when it comes to power either in position or in mental abilities.

One that should, with the present conditions, follow the now chosen profession and give to the peoples the results in occult, psychological and mystic forces through its endeavors in such work.

One who will find the greater success in present earth plane in such endeavors.

One who should be careful in its diet, for through digestion does the greater destructive force come to the physical.

Editor's Note: The following is a drawing guided by Cayce and includes an image of the sign and a description. It is part of a Life Seal that Cayce said would help the soul.

Reading 303-31 Atlantis Life Seal

Upon the left side put the outline, in a circle, of Atlantis. This would be near an outline of the continent now of Australia. In the center at the top of the outline of land put a red circle. About the circle, enclosing the map or outline of Atlantis, put four symbols of Leo. These would be in black, quite small. The color of the land, or Atlantis, would be gray-green.

Upon the right put the sign of the earth; this in blue-gray—this, to be sure, a circle also. About same would be the symbol of Libra.

The interpretation would be the desire of the soul-entity from Infinity into first activity in Atlantis, indicating in red the turmoil, indicating in the light of the earth journey. The symbols about same—Leo, Libra—represent the mental expansion in Leo—in Libra, the being too liberal, as would be literally expressed, with self.

Reading 4313-4

We find that the present entity took its flight from that position of Mercury and with Venus, and in the sign of Leo, that has much to do with the worries mentally of the body in the earth's plane. That is, the mental worries of the present entity has to do more with conditions that are of the mental, or head forces, as in Leo, and of the heart than other conditions.

With these conditions, then, we find this, irrespective of the will force as may be manifested in the present earth's plane:

One who has a good understanding of most any condition that may be presented, yet is found to differ with most of those who would be friendly toward the individual. Hence once that is often termed as being head-strong, self-willed, peculiar, fanatical, eccentric and such; yet these conditions are of the individual a certainty in their own mind. This, as we see, is produced by that element of experience through which the entity has passed in earthly sojourns.

VIRGO
Reading 365-3

As to the activities that are innate and manifested in the entity, coming in the constellation—or astronomical constellation activity—of Virgo:

At times the entity has the appearance of being self-sufficient in its relationships with individuals; hence it is often termed rather eccentric, especially so in the choosing of friendships and associates.

There is also a tendency for the reasoning of relationships; hence the entity is termed rather of the materialistic turn of mind. This also gives the entity in the present experience the ability to train or to conduct the training of the young mind; yet it is often found that the greater successes are from intuitional activities rather than from a set rule. From the very nature of the mental experiences and activities, these conditions make combative experiences in the entity's activities or associations in the present; causing the entity to continue to seek plans, ways, means, manners of ferreting out of the necessary connection for developments in such a field of activity.

Also, under Jupiterian influence, the entity has a broad vision of things, conditions, circumstances, peoples; hence it may be termed one with a wealth of knowledge. However, knowledge is not always power without the intelligence or an intelligent approach to make practical application of it, as the entity has oft experienced.

From the same influence we find that there will be periods in the entity's experience when there should be considerable of this world's goods to be controlled or directed by the entity. To be sure, this depends much upon the application of will's influence in the affairs of the entity.

Coming also under the influence of Venus, with the knowledge, with the vision, with the characterization of activities in the experience of the entity, peculiar situations have arisen and do arise in the love affairs of the entity in this particular experience; yet these, in a manner these influences, rather than the love affairs), control a great deal the activity of the entity; for, the entity is one that is tender-hearted, yet at some periods others feel that the entity is very rigid and unfeeling.

LIBRA
Reading 533-20
For instance, Aries indicates the mind—or the use of head; while Libra indicates the balance kept in body, mind and purpose in such an experience.

Reading 1710-3
There have been periods when the entity apparently has been blocked in the preparation for this or that activity, this or that association with individuals, and circumstances that would have changed or do change the whole course of events for the entity.

These influences all come from the Atlantean's activities that have brought Libra (of the balance) into force in such a manner that it might be said of the entity, indeed there is a path cut out for thee—the gods have directed that ye will have the opportunity to show forth thy worth.

Reading 1742-4

(Q) *Is my indecision of mind due to the qualities of Libra, or due also to a negative condition?*

(A) This, to the body, has almost answered itself already! for, as has been indicated, with the atomic forces as are active in every cell, or atom, or corpuscle, of the body, there is both the positive and the negative forces as apparent. Through the activities that one has acted in the material plane, through the entrance or sojourn in same, there have been inclinations created; as do environments or habits create inclinations in a physical body. So, as the body studies those inclinations as must arise from the activities of the sojourns in the earth's plane, as related to the present *experience* in the earth plane, these can be determined; but, as has been given oft, no force, no power in the earth, exceeds the *will* Force of God's highest creation—man! for man alone of all creation *defies* God! In those inclinations, then, let this become *apparent* in self: that with the better *understanding* of self, these will *enable* the body-consciousness, the mental—*being* of the body, to *make* self's will one with His Will, rather than gratifying any desire that has or does warp the mental-being or soul-consciousness in *any* manner. Hence that as was given, that "Ye have chosen Wisdom—I will give to thee *understanding* also." Let *this* imply to thine *own* activities. Do not excuse self. Meet *every* demand in Him, and He is able to not only aid but save, in the manner as will enable Him to magnify the Father in thee!

(Q) *Is my desire for mental independence correct, or somewhat self-centered?*

(A) As long as the dependence is in Him and not self, correct! When it becomes that "I *know*," irrespective, then it becomes self-centered; for, as was given, "Lord, God of hosts, be with us yet, *lest* I forget that *all force and* power *in* earth *or* heaven *comes from thee!* and in *each body* or mind I contact *is* one expressing their concept of *their* God!" Let the *answer*, then, of mental expedience, mental abilities, be in *Him*; and he that is wise *in Him* is wise indeed! He that is wise in self has *already* builded a barrier!

(Q) *Does my soul desire the impossible, or is it right for me to want only harmony and peace?*

(A) The whole of God's creation seeks harmony and peace! So, the desire of the soul for harmony and peace is born of Him that gave, "My peace I give unto thee;" not as the *world* gives peace, but as the *spirit* that makes alive that which gives the knowledge of *His* peace—that peace that passeth all understanding!

SCORPIO
Reading 2895-1

In taking the position in the present earth plane, we find this taken from those influences in Venus, with those of Uranus and of Mercury, with the adverse influence in Jupiter and in Mars, with the assistance in Saturn and in those of the Scorpio.

Then, we find those personalities given, as one by many considered peculiar in many ways; yet one whose dominant influence in the life is in the love as manifested to the body, and as the entity manifests to others; yet this brings, under some conditions, those influences that are at times (or have been in past) evil spoken of.

One that has lost much in the financial way, when there seemed almost impossible for things not to go just right.

One that has not always used discretion with better judgment.

One that has allowed small things, and influences of others, to over balance that judgement.

One slow of anger, yet capable of, through will's force, exercising that of grudge against others.

One that is slow of speech in many ways, and over abundance in speech in the single groups, on some questions.

One that should give to the world those manifestations of love's influence, for the entity should learn first that to *have* is to *give,* and the personalities as are exhibited are much of those urges as gained in appearances in the earth's plane. Some the entity gives voice to. Others remain as latent urges, and are as dreams, when the entity has builded to certain stages or positions in life.

Then, one not satisfied with the present occupation, and one that will, or should, change during the latter part of the present year, for these will, through these influences, as we see, bring that possibility for the entity. Then, use will forces, even though it may present at the time a form of unreasonableness, it will lend to the entity that ability of expansion that will build greater conditions in the life of this body.

As to the physical, as created in the present plane, its weaknesses being indigestion, and in the circulation, overtaxed through Scorpio, which is as the seat of the central portion of body, see?

The body, or entity, one of the eccentric intent, *by nature.*

One that loves to be something of a mystery to others—often *is,* to its own detriment.

One that is attracted to those of the beautiful in every way and manner.

One whose abilities lies greatest in that of the manufacturing end of any element that has to do with the product of the earth, and especially those that will be made into those conditions that may be as ornaments, or as beautiful, see?

Reading 5712–2

In the entrance into the earth's plane, we find the entity comes under the influence of Scorpio, Leo, and of Jupiter, Uranus, Mercury, and of Venus. Hence we find there are many contrariwise influences, as it were, in the influence in the present earth's plane—that is, many influences that, just when the entity would succeed in the physical plane, or in a physical manner, or in a material or financial manner, or in a social manner, or in social position, or in gaining for self fame, or in winning those things that come through the earthly influences, there seems to step in that something preventing the entity gaining the full benefits from same. Hence we find a life full of disappointments in many ways, yet those conditions that have to do with that benevolent influence in Jupiter, those eccentricities as have to do with those in Uranus, and those beloving influences as we find through that of Venus, often act as the saving grace, or day, as it were, for the entity.

Then, as to that personality as is exhibited in the present earth's plane:

One who holds every influence in the highest order.

One that brings much good to many.

One that is over true to friends, and may be ever counted upon to do that which is right and just in the eyes of all. Never belittling self, then, in any manner, save when seemingly bad judgement is taken, rather than the will to do that error.

In the influence, then, of Scorpio and of Leo, we find with those of Mercury, one of strong heart, strong willed, yet often weakened by bodily afflictions, and by accidents of the minor nature.

One, however, who will have many days in the present earth's plane, for the influences in the life, and the experiences in the present life, are such that will bring many days of usefulness, will the entity apply that knowledge as is being gained day by day.

As to the personal influence, irrespective of the will:

One we find of high mental character—one whose abilities in any field of endeavor requiring mental forces will succeed, yet the weaknesses in the flesh body often seem to hinder.

One who will find that there will come changes to the body in the present year. Being under the influence of Uranus and Jupiter, there will appear this change—these conditions, or those set about that will offer these changes, and be well for the entity to accept, about the 15th to 20th of October, in the present year.

SAGITTARIUS
Reading 779-5

Those influences under which this body come are those of Mercury, Venus and Jupiter, with phases of Venus forces giving afflictions. Those of Sagittarius also giving afflictions coming under the zodiacal sign of Aquarius. The influences then as we find come:

One well builded in body and mind, yet often under those Sagittarius forces that give the pains in physical to digestive tract and the head, when under the Aries sign with the Moon's phases. In the forces then we find will entering much in the developing to the present time.

One given to the love of the arts.

One given to the love of the social life in strange connections.

One given to the ennobling forces in the love of arts or of spiritual or soul elements.

One given to bring much joy to many peoples, in those especially in the sign of Scorpio and Gemini.

One that is above the normal in the forces as are manifest through Jupiter elements.

One that is destined to have many inconveniences in life's pathway by the conditions as presented in Venus under unfavorable conditions.

One that, however, in the ennobling influence of Jupiter's forces, with Mercury, finds much that will be builded upon those influences that have apparently been detrimental.

One that should ever keep in the straight and narrow way that leads to the developing of the soul and spirit forces in this present plane.

One whose greater force lies in giving the incentive to others to follow in that straight and narrow way that leads to the understanding of the One that gives Peace, Joy and Life to the World.

One whose vocation lies in that of the arts, and in the developing of others to understand the beauty of the soul and spirit forces of themselves.

CAPRICORN
Reading 630-2

In giving that which may be helpful to this entity in the present experience, respecting the sojourns in the earth, it is well that the planetary or astrological aspects also be given. It should be understood, then, that the sojourning of the soul in that environ, rather than the position, makes for the greater influence in the experience of an entity or body in any given plane. This is not belittling that which has been the study of the ancients, but rather it is giving the *understanding* of same. And, as we have indicated, it is not so much that an entity is influenced because the Moon is in Aquarius or the Sun in Capricorn or Venus or Mercury in that or the other house, sign, or the Moon and Sun sign, in that one of the planets is in this or that position in the heavens; but rather because those positions in the heavens are from the *entity* having been in that sojourn as a soul! This is how the planets have the greater influence in the earth upon the entity, see? For the application of an experience is that which makes for the development of a body, a mind, *or* a soul. For, how has it been written? "He that knows to do good and doesn't, to him it is sin." Then, the altering or changing factor in an influence is the application of the *will*, that which makes a soul, an entity—that dwells in that called man or woman (means the same)—capable, through this gift of the Creator, of being one with the Giver.

Then, in this entity, the experiences or sojourns in the environs in the earth's solar system are those things that make for *mental* urges innate and manifested, according to the *will of* the entity or body now known as [630].

We find Jupiter, then, as the greater ruling force; or the entity's sojourn in that environ. Not as a physical body as known in the earth, but as a body adaptable to the environs of Jupiter; for there's life there (not as known in earth), as there is in Saturn, Sun, Moon, Venus, Mercury, Uranus, Neptune, Mars; all have their form—as about the earth, the inhabitants of the air, fire, water—in and out of the earth. The elements about same are inhabited, if you choose, by those of their own peculiar environment.

We find Jupiter making for the experience in the present of the entity being an excellent executive in handling others, in looking after this or that character of associations of individuals with others—THROUGH the entity as the pilot or manager, or guide. And especially will the entity find, from that sojourn in the present experience, there will be brought marital life in the latter or middle portion of this experience; and in relationships with one whose dealings are with (or should be) wheat, grain, cereals, coffee, tea, or those things that have to do with the body-functioning of individuals, groups, masses, classes or nations. In this environ will the entity gain the better in such relationships.

In Jupiter we find also the abilities to meet individuals of every walk of life, to be associated in many environs and many activities of individuals in varied active experiences.

The influences from Mercury, with Uranus, make for the high mental abilities; and an individual, person or entity who may read character easily; thus adapting self—in the mental, the associations and the environs of associations—towards an executive, or as one who may direct the activities of others in their associations with individuals, especially as to such things as *collecting*—whether money or things, or those things that would deal with the individual life or affairs of individuals—even moneys. As insurance, banking, or the like. All of these come under these influences.

And as the psychic forces are manifested from the Uranian experience, it makes for an individual at times that is considered rather moody; or may be feeling wonderful in body, yet out of the influences may come those things that make for the willies, the blues, the jimmies, or the like, at times; or one that may be called very definite, yet at times very obstinate and at times very *indefinite* as to whether it will or whether it won't in whatever the relationships may be! Hence it often keeps not only the friends but the family, and even the male associates, *guessing* as to what will be the activities or the relationships; but this is an ability for a real executive, *provided* the entity or soul—in such relationships— knows *itself* what it is after—and the entity in its experience usually does!

Reading 849-1

In entering, we find the entity comes under the influence of Mercury, Uranus, Jupiter, Neptune, and with those influences in Capricorn and the Moon.

These conditions, as we find, make—as it were—many peculiar influences in the life of the entity, yet this should remain as that of the greater truth in this present experience: There is no influence in the life as great as the will of self; yet the entity may find these various urges in the present experience, for while these are as urges, many are of such a nature in the present experience, now, as to become the known factor with the entity, will self but [if self will but] apply or seek for the lessons for those particular urges as will be given in the life of the present.

Under the influence, then, in the Mercurian force or experience, there is seen that of exceptional mental abilities, with the love for the delving into those of mysteries of every nature, especially as pertaining to thought, mind, or those emanations from same. Almost to the point of that of the desire of closer biological study, yet just remaining in the realm rather of the mental, than of things. Then we find, with these influences, rather conditions are interesting and draw the individual, than *things* or peoples, save as they pertain *to* such mental developments.

In Jupiterian forces there are seen those ennobling conditions, that— weighed well grounded with the mental, and the exceptional conditions in the life—will find the needs of the entity being well grounded in that as the entity would set as the ideals; for without set ideals the entity—with the mental, and the love of mystery—may find self at the tangent, even to self's own purpose, and to the good and the peace of mind that may be even attained in this present experience.

Again we find that influence in the Venus' forces playing rather the important urge in the life in the twenty-fifty (25th) and sixth (6th) year. Well that same be weighed well with the ideas and ideals, and that same are not at an at-variance to the ideals and purposes set in self—for, as will be seen in that of the experiences of the entity in the earth's plane, these are as an element to be combated with; for in the last experience was the entity's undoing.

In that of the applications, then, of these urges:

Be not overcome with that of the desire, but overcome desire with purpose.

As is seen, there is then as these as manifested characteristics in the present experience, shown and called as personality, to many:

One high-minded, and rather of the ethereal turn—in the vision.

One that is attracted to few, yet attracts many.

One that makes friendships and chooses, rather, from same.

Considered, then, eccentric in a manner, and by others rather as the plain, well seeing, well meaning—yet not well grounded, varying according to the perspective, as it were, of purpose. Hence that injunction: Set thine *ideal* in Him, and *keep* same there!

One who feels that love is as something to be attained to, and to the entity, each individual must live to self's own ideal—and, as given, these will change. Hence, be sure same is set high.

Lover of the beautiful, whether in music, poetry, art, literature, or of the outdoors.

Lover of waters, lakes, and of nature as it may sing, or attune the self to higher, nobler, things.

One, then, with whom it is necessary for the *ideal* to be set *in* an ideal, and raise self to same.

AQUARIUS
Reading 256-1

In entering we find astrologically the entity coming under the influence of Aquarius and Venus, Jupiter, Mercury, and Neptune. Water will ever be a factor in this body's endeavors. The body should ever live near large bodies of water. Be more careful of those of high mountains or gorges, and of distant places.

In entering, we find the influences that give to the entity exceptional abilities in the present experience, in lines or individual factors. These, kept in the manner toward which the entity would apply will's influence, by keeping an *ideal*—not an idea—an *ideal*—before self, will build for self that which will carry the entity to where few, if any, appearances would be necessary again in this mundane sphere.

In the abilities as come through the influences in Aquarius, we find the entity could, or would, be able to apply self in influencing those that have to do with mathematical calculations, especially regarding aeronautics or boat building. The entity may become an architect beyond compare, provided these have to do with those elements that have to do with water or air.

Those influences in Jupiter and in Neptune bring for the entity those desire of study, those desires of loneliness; yet the life filled with those conditions that have to do with people. People and things, *both*, interest the entity. The barter and sale interest little. Moneys mean little to the entity, save as for that to procure that necessary in the affairs of everyday life. Rather those of character, and those of that that builds for an individual as to being their worth, and their worth to the entity meaning their ability to aid in given direction, or in giving to individuals or groups that which will aid them in making life either easier or more profitable—whether for moneys or for pleasures, or for own development.

In the likes and dislikes for this entity, these are apparently contradictory—for affection or love *rules* the life in many respects, yet little affection is shown, except in some directions—yet the deeper affection, as friendships, and love of individuals and of things, are to the entity of the same nature—yet these, builded in a manner, are better in the application in the present experience. To the entity friendships are strong. Dislikes are also strong, but the actions in dislikes are rather as if they did not exist, or as if individuals or things did not exist. The entity then is, in a manner, *not* a fatalist, yet activities would tend to make one believe such were the innate beliefs of the entity. Rather the love of the whole, or of the oneness of all force, gives that portion in the life that brings those conditions which build.

In the mathematical end of developments may the entity gain much, especially in study that has to do with the mystic, and the mysticism of numbers. These to the entity may be made much worth while. The entity may aid self, aid others, in the study of not only astrology but astronomy, and numbers as associated with same; aiding individuals in that, through that, that may be builded from character, as related to individual development, and the entity may then find that which will, may become, in THIS individual application of truths, that as the astrologer then for same, through numbers. Not through astrology alone. Rather numbers, and the application of numbers and numerology in its *deeper* sense. These are the elements that interest the entity. These may be worked out with mathematical precision in *many* individuals, yet applied with that as may be attained from an individual's life appliance—that is, the application of the individual towards life itself, or towards the entity's application of life in its own individuality, these may aid much in the establishing of truths in these directions.

Reading 1740-1

In entering we find the entity coming under the influence of Aquarius and the Moon, with Jupiter, Mercury, Venus influences in the experience of the entity. Mars as an affliction in the Moon, especially in the harvest seasons. Hence we find there have been conflicting experiences in the entity's sojourn in the present, as well as in the manner—or matter—of application of self as respecting those who were born especially under Sagittarius, or the early fall or harvest moon—September. In the present, many conflicting things, then, as given, and only an astrological aspect would be so conflicting as to be confusing, would the entity understand self in the present and make application of that as has been experienced and may be experienced . . .

In the influences seen in Aquarius, and the *detrimental* effects in Sagittarius—conflict, for while waters and great expanses of space call, in these the entity finds the most *quieting* of experiences; for in an experience as will be seen, and under circumstances when expanses and spaces brought the most contemplative experience of the mental being, did the entity gain most.

In those influences from Mars and Venus, these bring those sudden desires as regard physical relationships, bringing loves of a fiery nature within, and the seeking for the gratification of desires as respecting individuals; which, if guided aright, will yet bring in the experience OF the entity a body *through* which, *with* which, the entity may gain; not an *easiness*, but a surcease of a nature that will bring quiet and restfulness, and peace, in the experience of the entity. Be sure that such an one is of the fire nature, and that his *influences*—as periods—are in the fall, or October, and either a one and two, or two and two, or two and four.

Reading 122–1

[This soul birth into the Earth was] . . . taken from that of Venus, with the help of those influences from Mercury, Mars, Saturn and Uranus at times, with the assistance of Jupiter; afflictions coming in Moon's effect and in Sagittarius. Hence we have an individual, without respect will's manifestation in the present earth's plane, of exceptional abilities, and of many contradictory manifestations of the effects of planets, or of astrological conditions as has been considered and studied by peoples for many ages; yet, with that influence as will be seen through the correct interpretation of astrological effect in earth's development that would be manifest in the present entity, and the views as are held on life in earth plane, and the body's precept and concept of life and its effect, and the transmutation through the earthly sphere.

Then, without respect of the will, we have one given to be very much attracted to many peoples, of many climes, of many conditions, of many positions, of many phase of many actions. Hence the ability of the entity, when the influences of Mercury, especially, are considered, to gain much by what has been and is termed in physical plane as actual experience, and many learn *only* from such.

An entity that would be, and is, a wonderful study from the psychological and pathological viewpoint of the development in the mental and spiritual spheres, as manifest in the physical plane.

One given to study, read, much of other conditions, other positions, other experiences, of those in many spheres, especially those of royalty and their physical action in material world.

One that would be given to the study of anatomical or anatomic conditions, that have to do with the elements as of Venus persuasion.

In the elements, then, of that wherein the mental development, the spiritual environment through which the entity has passed in other spheres:

One who could have made a wonderful success in that as of the metaphysical physician.

One who may at present make a success in the study of those elements pertaining to vibration and the rejuvenation of physical forces in human anatomy, that may be revived by elements (physical) of vibration.

In the development, we have many phases through which entity has passed in earth's plane, coming in contact with many of the elements of purely physical carnal plane, in contact with many of the mental and spiritual and soul plane. The entity may develop, yet, far in those forces pertaining to the occult forces, for with the present development in the earth's plane, and with the renewed elements as are manifest in earth's plane, through influence of Uranian forces in earth's plane, in the next six to thirteen months the entity may gain much of knowledge that will bring better conditions for self and for others, giving then an understanding that would, will the will but manifest in that manner in assisting others.

Reading 1222-1

As to the influences that arise from the astrological sojourns, these are rather in keeping with the time—the Aquarius forces, and as there are the beginnings of the Aquarian age.

Then *do not* consider self as being unusual because unusual experiences arise in thy associations, in thy meditations, in thy activities with thy fellow men. Do not do *other*, though, than contemplate these. Remember thou art in the same signs, omens, as the Mother of Him; that gave to the earth the physical man, Jesus—Aquarius in its *perception*, perfection.

Hence when those experiences arose in that life, ye find it said, "She pondered these in her heart."

Hence the same injunction might be given. For no better direction can be had or given than the consecrating of self in body, in mind, in activity to the service of those influences, those forces that may be as those that the self may give to others in the meditations, in the supplications; keeping self in those directions that *indeed* as He gave, "Ye abide in me, I in the Father," and ye may know those forces from the abiding presence of the Master's forces.

As to those forces that arise from Venus, from the sojourns of the entity there, we find that emotions of a nature—yet spiritual emotions rather than the body emotions—make for ruling influences in the life. Yet keep *these* coordinant. For know that there *is* a way at times that seemeth right yet the end is confusion—unless it be directed by those forces, those influences as arise from direction by the application of the spirit of truth; as in patience, long-suffering, charity, fellowship, grace and mercy.

For it will be seen that a greater and greater controlling force may be obtained in self by being *quiet* within, listening to the still small voice as may speak from within the temple where He hath promised ever to meet those that seek to know Him.

Turn then oft within, that those forces of love, those influences of patience, those activities even of long-suffering, may bear with those that make for even heartaches from the misinterpretation of their activities; but directing of such, as in the relationships in the home, may oft be better done by prayer than by tirade ever!

Those forces as we find from the astrological aspects in Uranus make for the extremes in the experiences of the *association*, rather than in self. For as self *has* been, as self *is* well balanced in its ideas and ideal, to such an individual there oft appears to be much that makes for turmoils or indecisions in the minds or activities at least of others.

Hence keep *quiet* and at peace within, and we will find extremes becoming *means* and ways and manners and activities that are befitting those that set their ideals in the spiritual forces.

Those aspects as we find from Neptune make for those experiences that will be rather as the dealings with many that have to do with water, the *sources* of influence or force in materiality.

Hence we will find material means, material sustenance, oft may come from the fruits of waters; or as those relationships across many waters. These bring then an influence that may needs be reckoned with, yet hold fast to that faith in Him. For as He is, was, holy; so may ye be holy in Him.

For He hath promised to be thy counsel, thy guard, thy stay, and a very present help in trouble.

Remember Him also then in thy joys as well as thy sorrows, remembering Him also in thy displeasures as well as thy pleasures. For where the heart is there the treasure will be also.

Reading 1265-1

In the astrological aspects, then, we find these are those environments:

Aquarius—making for the application of the mental self. Thus in Mercury we find the high mental abilities of the entity. And with those tendencies to analyze any given project, any given undertaking that may deal with the material world. Though the more oft the entity undertakes projects or undertakings when *others* should be considered *with* the entity, and a *cooperative* spirit manifested by the entity in doing so. Not that what is conceived or undertaken in the mental forces of the entity is not well, but these come upon hard experiences for the lack of cooperation with those with whom the entity might or may become affiliated or associated in material undertakings . . .

Learn these, my brother: If ye would have friends, show thyself friendly! If you would have love, show thyself lovely in the *little* things as well as in the mass or in the larger things. That ye give, that ye have. If it has been, then, of material things—these become as *cold*, stark, blank. If it has been love, if it has been friendship, if it has been grace, mercy, long-suffering, brotherly love—these grow, these bloom, even in a material world; and the fruits thereof are joy, happiness, peace and understanding, and bring to an entity, an individual, the worth while experiences of a sojourn in the earth.

Then from this same we find those tendencies for the interests in the mystic, the psychic, the occult forces. *Do not confuse them!* For that as becomes applicable in thine experience must be prompted by the desire, the wish within self, and that in accordance with divine ideals.

What, then, *is* thine ideal? Is it founded in that ye yourself may do, or that in which ye may be the *channel* through which others may find *their* association with a *living* God, a living ideal, a living love, a living faith, a living experience of joy? *These* be they which are of the truth, and thus grow as does the spirit of truth.

PISCES
Reading 2082-1

As to the urges which are latent and manifested, we find these coming under the astrological aspects of Pisces; making for a very intuitive force—and this is well, but do not magnify same in letting the imaginations oft override the better judgements in thy relationships to others. If such intuitive urges are kept in a spiritual import, they will grow to be helpful rather than antagonizing influences.

Reading 2115-1

Pisces' influence brings those conditions, as has been the experience in the present, as will be the experience through that to come, where definite decisions must be made by self, that alter not only the surroundings and environs but the adaptability of self to those sudden changes that come in the experience of the entity.

Reading 2123-2

Venus—with the love influence, and Pisces bringing a variation in the aspects of the entity as an influence conflicting with those of the April influence, that makes for contrarywise experiences, and when the entity as a developing being in the present has allowed that of the influence that makes for madness in Mars, there has come those detrimental things that make for an *unbalancing* of the entity's outlook upon the present experience, as well as doubt and fear for that as has been or may be.

Reading 2124-3

One, as in Aries, that has a mind of his own, and expresses same at times to where some would call the entity tending towards hardheaded, or a man of his own mind. This has been altered much by the application of will as respecting same, so that those influences as come in Pisces, from the close associations of the entity as respecting its influ-

ence, has altered to that where rather *judgement*, discretion, has often
been the balancing power as respecting such conditions; yet one that
thinks first before he speaks, and this has been builded also by those
influences in Mars, as with Venus, Jupiter, Mercury, bringing for the
entity many a varied and many a wide vision of experience in the mental world, in the material affairs, and in those things as pertain to the
spiritual, or spirituality in the life of the entity.

Reading 2137-1

In Pisces' influence we find those of the mystic forces have their influence and *interest* for the body, in that *manner* as is influenced through
those forces in Venus—as make for a manifestation of same as love's
influence.

Hence the religious turn of thought for the entity, but far from being
dogmatic in its attitude or application; rather in that of the broader sense.

Reading 2205-1

The Piscean influence makes for the mystery, the mysterious; and oft
those who study or attempt to analyze the entity find that it is in its
characteristics of that nature and temperament. Then, these bring those
astrological influences of extremes—of beauty and of mathematical precision. Hence the entity is a mathematician; and these—mathematics
with sympathy, with other tendencies—apparently become conflicting.

Reading 2282-1

The spiritual interpretation of the signs of the zodiac, as in Pisces, is
that the entity has sought and does seek so often in its dealings and in
its relationships to others.

Hence in material manifestation the entity finds an interest in things
and conditions that may be spoken of as concerning psychic or spiritual things. Let the greater interpretation of the word psychic to the self,
to the souls of men, be rather as the soul forces of men than their
disincarnate beings! For, as ye live and move and have thy being in and
through the grace of the Creator, so may it indeed be true that whether
ye live or whether ye pass into the other chambers of God's universe, ye
are indeed His!

Reading 2322-2

Under Pisces are the active forces; thus those things which have to do with water, or that depend upon water, will be channels through which activities in this material plane will be of a greater interest to the entity. Not necessarily ships, or things in water, but things that depend upon water as a portion of their activity, or their development.

Reading 2339-1

In the astrological aspects these are latent and manifested urges, as the period indicated under the Piscean; thus giving a religious or a routine thought.

Thus as a rhymist, or as a householder, as a writer, the entity finds the surroundings at times vague. And for this the entity finds self condemned at times; and this is—and has been—covered up in disappointments.

8

Two Soul-Life Examples

Example One

Reading 910-4 Female

Mrs. Cayce: You will give the relation of this entity and the universe, and the universal forces; giving the conditions which are as personalities, latent and exhibited in the present life; also the former appearances in the earth plane; giving time, place and the name, and that in each life which built or retarded the development for the entity; giving the abilities of the present entity, that to which it may attain, and how. You will answer the questions, as I ask them.

Mr. Cayce: (In going back over years from the present—" '37—changes as came—'35-'27—yes, changes and awakenings—'25—" etc., on back to birth date.)

Yes, we have the records here of that entity now known as or called–[910].

In giving the interpretations of the records as we find them, these are chosen with the desire and purpose that this may be a helpful experience for the entity; enabling the entity to fill that purpose for which it entered this present experience; that there may be the magnifying of the virtues, minimizing of the faults; and thus make the glory of the purpose as one with that consciousness which brings the awareness of activities in this experience.

Very unusual, in manners, are some of the influences about the entity, other than that ordinarily indicated in astrological aspects or in material sojourns.

The life pattern or seal is rather unique; in that it partakes of both the old and the new, and of all of those activities of various series or periods of development.

It is a wreath with a streamer; the center with the hieroglyphics of El in Hebrew character (meaning God); while the background and all about the wreath should be of myrtle and berries, indicating the outdoors. The wreath would be of the beech leaf, rather than the maple; also beech in color and in shape, you see. The center would be gold, of course, while the background would be the light blue, or sky blue. This as we find will be interpreted from the sojourns of the entity in the earth, and the variations of the entity's appearance and activity in the material plane.

Astrologically we find Venus, Mercury, Jupiter, Uranus the ruling forces and influences. Though Saturn is not a beneficent influence, it is not an influence for the changes as sometimes—or the more often—indicated through activities or sojourns there.

In Venus we find the home and the beauties of friendships; with Uranus as well as Mercury bringing about influences of wisdom, strength, and unseen influence among groups of masses through which the entity may—and does—influence others.

This almost becomes then an unconscious influence that the entity bears.

In Uranus with Saturn we find the desire, latent and manifested, to be alone often; fearful of little or nothing, save of hurting others' feelings, or of those things as would pertain to others.

The hope and the dreaming in regard to the mysterious influences or occult forces, by nature the entity is attracted to these, as well as this being latent in the inmost influence of the entity.

One whose abilities in the home, as well as in the associations with others, influence activities towards things pertaining to adornment, outdoor activities, as well as pertaining to manners and means of influencing other individuals.

As to the appearances of the entity in the earth, we find that these have been quite varied (as indicated from the seal), and touch—or are influencing from—many stations or periods of activity and development.

Before this the entity was in the land of the present nativity, entering almost immediately from another appearance. Unusual! The desire for expression of self being hindered in the Norse land, the entity passing *suddenly* sought expression.

Thus we find the entity entered the land of the present nativity, as an Indian maiden, though wedded to one of the white race; and making an ideal home for those of that period, in that region which lies between what is now Yorktown and Williamsburg.

Because of its early return, the entity's activities there were in the influencing of its own peoples, as well as its companion and the activities through same, as to manners and means of preserving or producing the great economic activities among the peoples; for the saving of the fruit of the soil, fruit of the land, fruit of the peoples in their mental as well as spiritual undertaking.

Thus we find that the entity gained throughout that experience; yet bringing into the present experience an air or a mien oft that is not wholly understood by others. Yet most of those who are even acquaintances of the entity would be the gainers to pattern much of their relationships to others by this entity! For, it tends to its own affairs, and helps or aids others in those periods and times when questions may arise.

The abilities in the economic activities pertaining to all phases of human relationships arise from that sojourn.

Then the entity was first known as Bluebird; later, with the associations in the home and in the activities among the associates, as Clara Bowden; and there is still a record of that, in the hills—but it's in the woods mightily now.

Before that the entity was in the Norse land, as indicated, when there were those becoming active in journeys to other lands.

The entity then was among those of the Olaf family, and saw the companion and those of its own household leave without returning. The desire to know their fate, to follow irrespective of what was said or given concerning others, soon brought the separation from the physical and mental to the spiritual forces.

It may be said that the entity gained and lost in the experience; *gained* because of devotion, lost because of that made in the experience of others—a selfish one. These become influences, then, that the entity must combat.

Do not become self-centered; and refrain from condemning self (as you do oft).

Before that the entity was in the land when the Master walked in the earth; when there were those activities about Galilee; and when there was the entering in and the calling of the Disciples about Peter's home.

The entity was among those who were present and saw Peter's mother-in-law healed. This to the entity, then, has never been as a mystery—instantaneous healing. While never fully understood, there is the belief and the willingness to act in that direction without questioning; which is latent and manifested as a part of the entity—to be sincere, to be in the house of faith.

In the experience the entity knew many material hardships, and many of those activities to which those of the faith were called through persecution by those in the political as well as social activities.

Hence in the present we find the entity disregarding social relations, so much as the real *purposes* of the individual activity and influence.

The name then was Ruth; and *well* is the name for the entity in the present. The entity was a niece then of Peter, but *not* Andrew's daughter—rather the daughter of Barjon.

Before that the entity was in those activities when there was the returning of the children of promise to the Holy Land; when there were the preparations for the renewing of the service in the temple.

It was when there was the reestablishing of those activities there under Zerubbabel and Ezra and Nehemiah. All of these were acquaintances of the entity, but Zerubbabel was the closer relationship—for the entity was his daughter-in-law.

The name then was Jephtha. In the experience the entity set the example for the mothers in that period, by the establishing—in the homes of those who returned to the city—the teaching centers for the children, for the making known of the awareness of the law as well as the ordinances, as well as the meanings of those things which had been estab-

lished by Aaron and Moses and the earlier priests—as Eleazar and (?)
[Eder?]. All of these were the lessons the entity taught; thus El (meaning
God), but in the Hebrew character as the center of the wreath in the
entity's seal.

From that experience in the present we find the great love of data,
facts, pertaining to activities of individuals, and many of those things
especially pertaining to the size of this or that, the weight that meant
this or that, the length of the tunic or coat or breeches of the priests—all
have a special interest. For, the entity had much to do with the preparing of these at that period.

Before that the entity was in the Egyptian land, during those periods
when there were the turmoils and strifes, and when there was the ejec-
tion or banishment of the Priest.

The entity was among those in the land to which the priest and those
with him were banished. The entity came under those activities, those
influences, and returned to the Egyptian land; near to the areas in which
there was the great pyramid and city; and one that is yet to be uncov-
ered—in a portion of that just beyond the Great Pyramid—was the home
of the entity in the latter portion of its sojourn there; a home magnifi-
cent, for it was turned to a place where preparations were made for
those of both sexes, for their preparations as children, for the activities
through the Temple of Sacrifice and the Temple Beautiful.

Then the entity was closely associated with the activities of the Priest,
as well as those who coordinated and cooperated with the Priest in
establishing the customs in the land.

The name then was Is-Ar-Ar-Ra. The experience, then, was one of
growth and activity, and one from which the entity may draw much in
the present; knowing that as ye build in the experiences of others by
counsel, advice, and by the living of same in self, ye are measuring up
to that which brings the at-onement as attained in that experience.

As to the abilities of the entity in the present, then:

Study to show thyself approved unto that ideal that ye hold, as ye
held in that companionship with the Apostles, as ye held particularly as
the high priestess in Egypt; and keep self from condemning self, or from
doubting self's own abilities.

These are the ways—His ways.

Ready for questions.

(Q) *What should be my life's work?*

(A) Helping or aiding others to find themselves.

(Q) *What line of work should I follow in order to care for myself and son?*

(A) Anything that would have to do with clothing or adorning, whether in selling or in making or designing.

(Q) *Please give me some advice that will help me in training my son.*

(A) Rather would the sources seek advice from thee! Thou hast within thyself that which takes hold upon the very truths as He expressed. These as precepts, as examples, are the way.

(Q) *What can I do to help him have a strong, healthy body?*

(A) Follow those counsels that will bring the life-giving forces and influences into the experience of the body.

(Q) *Would it be well for all concerned, especially my son, for me and my husband again to resume our marriage relation?*

(A) This must be decided within self. As ye would that others would do, do ye even so to them.

(Q) *Is there any special jewelry that I should wear?*

(A) Anything that is of the nature of the coral wreath, or that is made in the form of wreaths—either of enamel or the filigree. These especially are well.

(Q) *To what colors do I vibrate best?*

(A) Mauve.

(Q) *Where, and in what capacity, have I been associated in former experiences with members of Group #2 of Norfolk, Va? First, Mrs. [379]?*

(A) These can be best drawn by comparisons; for where there are associations, or paralleling of same, it may be seen. We find at least two, and these were very closely associated in those experiences.

(Q) *Mrs. [404]?*

(A) The same; the Norse land as well as others.

(Q) *Miss [307]?*

(A) We find only one as a close association. Draw these from comparisons.

(Q) *How may I be of the most help to my mother . . . in this experience?*

(A) *Keeping* her glad! This may sound very broad, but to the entity it is not so broad.

We are through for the present.

Example Two

Reading 987-4 Female
Mrs. Cayce: You will have before you the entity, [987], present in this room, who seeks a Mental and Spiritual Reading, with information, advice and guidance as to her development and proper expression in the earth. You will answer the questions she submits, as I ask them:
Mr. Cayce: Yes, we have the entity, [987].

In giving the analysis of the mental and spiritual self, many are the conditions that arise as questions in the experience of the entity. These to be sure must be approached as to the purpose and the desires of the *spiritual* self.

That there may be a more perfect understanding, much as to those that have been the experiences of the entity as a soul-entity must be referred to.

For, life—or the motivative force of a soul—is eternal; and that portion of same that is motivated by the mental and spiritual attributes of an entity has experienced, does experience the influences that have guided or prompted same through its sojourns.

For each soul seeks expression. And as it moves through the mental associations and attributes in the surrounding environs, it gives out that which becomes either for selfish reactions of the own ego—to express—or for the *I Am* to be at-one with the Great *I Am that I Am.*

What then are the purposes for the activities of an entity in a material plane, surrounded with those environs that make for self-expressions or self-activities in the various ways and manners?

What meaneth these? That self is growing to that which it, the entity, the soul, is to present, as it were, to the Great *I Am* in those experiences when it is absent from materiality.

These become hard at times for the individual to visualize; that the mental and soul may manifest without a physical vehicle. Yet in the deeper meditations, in those experiences when those influences may arise when the spirit of the Creative Force, the universality of soul, of mind—not as material, not as judgments, not *in* time and space but *of* time and space—may become lost in the Whole, instead of the entity being lost in the maze of confusing influences—then the soul visions arise in the meditations.

And the centers becoming attuned to the vibrations of the bodily force, these give a vision of that as may be to the entity an outlet for the self-expressions, in the beauties and the harmonies and the activities that become, in their last analysis; just being patient, long-suffering, gentle, kind. *These* are the fruits of the spirit of truth; just as hates, malice and the like become in their growths those destructive forces in creating, in making for those things that are as but tares, confusions, dissensions in the experiences of an entity.

Those then are the purposes of the entrance of an entity into a material plane; to choose that which is its ideal.

Then ask thyself the question—gain the answer first in thy physical consciousness:

"What is my ideal of a *spiritual* life?"

Then when the answer has come—for it has been given by Him that is Life, that the kingdom of God, the kingdom of heaven, is within; and we view the kingdom of God without by the application of those things that are of the spirit of truth—These then answered, ye seek again in the inner consciousness:

"Am I true to my ideal?"

These become then the answers. This and that and the other; never as pro and con. For the growth in the spirit is as He has given; ye *grow* in grace, in knowledge, in understanding.

How? As ye would have mercy shown thee, ye show mercy to those that even despitefully use thee. If ye would be forgiven for that which is contrary to thy own purposes—yet through the vicissitudes of the experiences about thee, anger and wrath give place to better judgment—ye, too, will forgive those that have despitefully used thee; ye will hold no malice. For ye would that thy Ideal, that Way ye seek, hold no malice—yea, no judgment—against thee. For it is the true law of recompense; yea, the true law of sacrifice.

For not in sacrifice alone has He sought His judgments, but rather in mercy, in grace, in fortitude; yea, in divine love.

The shadows of these are seen in thy inner experience with thy fellow man day by day. For ye have seen a smile, yea a kind word, turn away wrath. Ye have seen a gentleness give hope to those that have lost their hold on purpose, other than the satisfying of an appetite—yea, other than satisfying the desires of the carnal mind.

Hence as ye give, ye receive. For this is mercy, this is grace.

This is the beauty of the inner life lived.

Know then it is not that judgment is passed here or there. For know that God looketh upon the heart and He judgeth rather the purposes, the desires, the intents.

For what seekest thou to lord (laud) in thy life? Self-intent? Know ye not that it was selfishness that separated the souls from the spirit of life and light? Then only in the divine love do ye have the opportunity to become to thy fellow man a saving grace, a mercy, yea even a savior.

For until ye have in thy own material associations known thyself to be the saving grace to someone, ye may not know even the whole mercy of the Father with the children of men.

Then it is not of rote; it is not ritual that has made for those influences in thine own experience; but in whom, in what hast thou put thy trust?

He has promised to meet thee within the temple of thine own body. For as has been given, thy body is the temple of the living God; a tabernacle, yea, for thy soul. And in the holy of holies within thine own consciousness He may walk and talk with thee.

Is it the bringing of sacrifice? Is it the burning of incense? Is it the making of thyself of no estate?

Rather is it that ye *purpose!* For the try, the purpose of thine inner self, to *Him* is the righteousness. For He hath known all the vicissitudes of the earthly experience. He hath walked through the valley of the shadow of death. He hath seen the temptations of man from every phase that may come into thine own experience; and, yea, He hath given thee, "If you will love me, believing I am able, I will deliver thee from that which so easily besets thee at *any* experience."

And it is thus that He stands; not as a Lord but as thy Brother, as thy Savior; that ye may know indeed the truth that gentleness, kindness, patience, brotherly love, beget—in thy heart of hearts, with Him—that peace, that harmony. Not as the world knoweth peace but as He gave:

"That peace I give ye; that ye may know that thy spirit, yea thy soul, beareth witness with me that ye are mine—I am thine," even as the Father, the Son, the Holy Spirit.

Even so may thy soul, thy mind, thy body, become aware of that which renews the hope, the faith, the patience within thee.

And until ye show forth in His love that patience, ye cannot become aware of thy relationship with Him. Even as He has given, in patience ye become aware of being that soul—that seeketh the Father's house that is within even thine own consciousness.

How? How, then, may ye approach the throne?

Turn thou within. As ye meditate, give forth in thine *own* words these thoughts:

"Father, God, Maker of heaven and earth! I am Thine—Thou art mine! As I claim that kinship with that holy love, keep Thou me in that consciousness of Thy presence abiding with me: that I may be that channel of blessings to others, that I may know Thy grace, Thy mercy, Thy love—even as I show such to my fellow man!"

And ye may be very sure the answer comes within.

Thus, as ye apply—the answer comes. Not—by applying do we mean—a separation from the world. For even as He, ye are *in* the world but not *of* the world. But putting away the worldly things ye take hold upon the spiritual things, knowing that the worldly are but the shadows of the real.

And thus, as ye come into the light of His countenance, it maketh thy heart glad in the consciousness of *"I am Thine—Thou art mine"* . . .

(Q) *What was the exact time of my soul birth?*

(A) Only a few breaths after the physical birth. For as has been indicated to the soul, in the experiences in the earth—how beautiful have been thy joys, yea even thy sorrows, that they have kept alive that longing for a closer communion, a closer walk with Him!

And as the soul came then with a purposefulness, that "I—even I—may be able to show forth His love among those I meet day by day," there was no tarrying. For ye are learning, ye have gained, ye may apply, *"As ye sow, so shall ye reap."*

For God is not mocked. Though man may separate himself, it is against the purposes, the will of the love of truth. And only self may separate thee from the love of the Father. For He longeth, even as thy soul crieth out in the mornings, "Holy—holy art Thou, O Lord!"

(Q) *If possible, what can I do to finish my earth's experience in this life?*

(A) It is ever possible. Studying to show forth the Lord's death till He come again!! What meaneth this?

Just living those that are the fruits of the spirit; namely: peace, harmony, long-suffering, brotherly love, patience. *These,* if ye show them forth in thy life, in thy dealings with thy fellow man, grow to be what? *Truth!* In truth ye are *free,* from what? *Earthly* toil, *earthly* cares!

These then are not just axioms, not just sayings, but *living* truths!

Ye are happy in His *love! Hold* fast to that!

(Q) *What is holding back my spiritual development?*

(A) Nothing holding back—as has just been given—but *self.* For know, as has been given of old, "Though I take the wings of the morning in thought and fly unto the uttermost parts of the earth, Thou art there! Though I fly into the heavenly hosts, Thou art there! Though I make my bed in hell, Thou art there!"

And as He has promised, "When ye cry unto me, I *will hear*—and answer speedily." Nothing prevents—only self. Keep self and the shadow away. Turn thy face to the light and the shadows fall behind.

(Q) *Please explain the meaning of a light I saw on the night of June 13th-14th, and a figure that appeared in the light.*

(A) These are but the beginnings of that which may be thy experience. This followed a deep meditation, though much broke in between. But it is the fruit of not thought, but purpose, desire. For it has not entered the heart of man all the glories that have been prepared, nor all the beauties that may be experienced by those that seek His face.

These are but the signs, yea the *assurances,* that His presence abideth with thee.

Know He hath promised that if ye ask, ye shall receive. Be satisfied only then with the consciousness of His presence. Who? That in Whom you have believed—that abides with thee. For "If ye will knock, I will open—for I stand at the door and knock."

If ye will but open thy tabernacle of consciousness to allow the holy to come in and sup with thee, yea *all* the beauties of peace and harmony *are* thine; for they are the birthright of each soul. For the soul is the portion of the Maker that makes thee individual, yet with the consciousness of being one with *God*, the *universe*, the *love*—that which *is* beauty and harmony.

(Q) *What is the meaning of the white lightning I have seen?*

(A) That awakening that is coming. More and more as the white light comes to thee, more and more will there be the awakening. For as the lights are in the colors: In the green, healing; in the blue, trust; in the purple, strength; in the white, the light of the throne of mercy itself. Ye may never see these save ye have withheld judgment or shown mercy.

(Q) *What is my worst fault?*

(A) What is ever the worst fault of each soul? *Self—self!*

What is the meaning of self? That the hurts, the hindrances are hurts to the self-consciousness; and these create what? Disturbing forces, and these bring about confusions and faults of every nature.

For the only sin of man is *selfishness!*

(Q) *How may it be overcome?*

(A) Just as has been given; showing mercy, showing grace, showing peace, long-suffering, brotherly love, kindness—even under the most *trying* circumstances.

For what is the gain if ye love those *only* that love thee? But to bring hope, to bring cheer, to bring joy, yea to bring a smile again to those whose face and heart are bathed in tears and in woe, is but making that divine love *shine—shine*—in thy own soul!

Then *smile*, be joyous, be glad! For the day of the Lord is at hand.

Who is thy Lord? Who is thy God?

Self? Or Him in Whom ye live and move and have thy being—that is *all* in *all*, God the Father, the Love—the *great* Hope, the Great Patience?

These are thy *all.*

Keep in the way that is arising before thee, more and more. And as ye open thy consciousness to the Great Consciousness within, there will arise more and more the white light.

For He is the light, and the life—eternal.

A.R.E. PRESS

Edgar Cayce (1877–1945) founded the non-profit Association for Research and Enlightenment (A.R.E.) in 1931, to explore spirituality, holistic health, intuition, dream interpretation, psychic development, reincarnation, and ancient mysteries—all subjects that frequently came up in the more than 14,000 documented psychic readings given by Cayce.

Edgar Cayce's A.R.E. provides individuals from all walks of life and a variety of religious backgrounds with tools for personal transformation and healing at all levels—body, mind, and spirit.

A.R.E. Press has been publishing since 1931 as well, with the mission of furthering the work of A.R.E. by publishing books, DVDs, and CDs to support the organization's goal of helping people to change their lives for the better physically, mentally, and spiritually.

In 2009, A.R.E. Press launched its second imprint, 4th Dimension Press. While A.R.E. Press features topics directly related to the work of Edgar Cayce and often includes excerpts from the Cayce readings, 4th Dimension Press allows us to take our publishing efforts further with like-minded and expansive explorations into the mysteries and spirituality of our existence without direct reference to Cayce specific content.

A.R.E. Press/4th Dimension Press
215 67th Street
Virginia Beach, VA 23451

Learn more at EdgarCayce.org. Visit ARECatalog.com to browse and purchase additional titles.

ARE PRESS.COM

EDGAR CAYCE'S A.R.E.

Who Was Edgar Cayce?
Twentieth Century Psychic and Medical Clairvoyant

Edgar Cayce (pronounced Kay-Cee, 1877-1945) has been called the "sleeping prophet," the "father of holistic medicine," and the most-documented psychic of the 20th century. For more than 40 years of his adult life, Cayce gave psychic "readings" to thousands of seekers while in an unconscious state, diagnosing illnesses and revealing lives lived in the past and prophecies yet to come. But who, exactly, was Edgar Cayce?

Cayce was born on a farm in Hopkinsville, Kentucky, in 1877, and his psychic abilities began to appear as early as his childhood. He was able to see and talk to his late grandfather's spirit, and often played with "imaginary friends" whom he said were spirits on the other side. He also displayed an uncanny ability to memorize the pages of a book simply by sleeping on it. These gifts labeled the young Cayce as strange, but all Cayce really wanted was to help others, especially children.

Later in life, Cayce would find that he had the ability to put himself into a sleep-like state by lying down on a couch, closing his eyes, and folding his hands over his stomach. In this state of relaxation and meditation, he was able to place his mind in contact with all time and space—the universal consciousness, also known as the super-conscious mind. From there, he could respond to questions as broad as, "What are the secrets of the universe?" and "What is my purpose in life?" to as specific as, "What can I do to help my arthritis?" and "How were the pyramids of Egypt built?" His responses to these questions came to be called "readings," and their insights offer practical help and advice to individuals even today.

The majority of Edgar Cayce's readings deal with holistic health and the treatment of illness. Yet, although best known for this material, the sleeping Cayce did not seem to be limited to concerns about the physical body. In fact, in their entirety, the readings discuss an astonishing 10,000 different topics. This vast array of subject matter can be narrowed down into a smaller group of topics that, when compiled together, deal with the following five categories: (1) Health-Related Information; (2) Philosophy and Reincarnation; (3) Dreams and Dream Interpretation; (4) ESP and Psychic Phenomena; and (5) Spiritual Growth, Meditation, and Prayer.

Learn more at EdgarCayce.org.

What Is A.R.E.?

Edgar Cayce founded the non-profit Association for Research and Enlightenment (A.R.E.) in 1931, to explore spirituality, holistic health, intuition, dream interpretation, psychic development, reincarnation, and ancient mysteries—all subjects that frequently came up in the more than 14,000 documented psychic readings given by Cayce.

The Mission of the A.R.E. is to help people transform their lives for the better, through research, education, and application of core concepts found in the Edgar Cayce readings and kindred materials that seek to manifest the love of God and all people and promote the purposefulness of life, the oneness of God, the spiritual nature of humankind, and the connection of body, mind, and spirit.

With an international headquarters in Virginia Beach, Va., a regional headquarters in Houston, regional representatives throughout the U.S., Edgar Cayce Centers in more than thirty countries, and individual members in more than seventy countries, the A.R.E. community is a global network of individuals.

A.R.E. conferences, international tours, camps for children and adults, regional activities, and study groups allow like-minded people to gather for educational and fellowship opportunities worldwide.

A.R.E. offers membership benefits and services that include a quarterly body-mind-spirit member magazine, Venture Inward, a member newsletter covering the major topics of the readings, and access to the entire set of readings in an exclusive online database.

Learn more at EdgarCayce.org.

EDGARCAYCE.ORG